What Others Are Saying

I've known Pastor Mark close to ten years. He is a servant with a generous heart to help others achieve something significant. In this manuscript that Mark has penned, his desire to assist others continues to ring through loud and clear. It is in Mark's DNA to flow in this realm.

There is a reference in Chapter 4 about blind spot's while driving a vehicle. I don't think any of us know, how often we have near-miss accidents, looking over our shoulder before making a turn, or switching lanes. So, it is with our lives; we can avoid so much potential pain and anguish if we will look, see, and respond to our blind spots. If we don't deal with our blind spots, they can cloud our vision to the point that we miss the Light of God trying to connect us to healing, deliverance, and restoration.

Mark has written personal stories and has also included healing stories that demonstrate the power and love of Jesus that illustrate the points he is making in each chapter. Some of his childhood tales are outrageous, such as being a young boy trying to jump off the roof of his house while using a bed sheet as a parachute. Another story finds him pretending to be Tarzan while jumping from a dump truck, only to be stabbed in the mouth by a pointed object.

Keep a pencil or pen in hand to make personal notes as you delve into the text and to fill in the blanks provided within. Be ready for God to speak to you and to show areas of your life, and then be quick to respond and allow the Lord to restore anything that Satan has stolen. You can trust the author of this book and the author of your faith as you proceed.

-- **Jay West,** pastor and author of the books: *Kingdom Encounters, Downloads From Heaven, Willing To Yield,* and *Well, Well, Well.*

Pastor Mark Baxter's book, *Discover Your Blind Spots*, is unique and compelling. Mark has a gift of articulating things that other people may avoid, such as blind spots, which are important to bring to light. His approach is clear, concise, and easy to apply. In addition to his being a good teacher and pastor, he has a gift to bring freedom to the body of Christ by addressing areas that we often don't see, and don't know how to receive healing from them. His teaching and practical steps towards deliverance and healing through the power of the Holy Spirit will bring new life to all those that avail themselves to his wisdom.

> -- **Cindy Hasz,** LVN, CMC, President/CEO, *Grace Care Management*

DISCOVER YOUR BLIND SPOTS

Rid Yourself of Relational Time Bombs

Mark Baxter

© Copyright 2018 Mark Baxter

All rights reserved. No part of this publication may be reproduced or transmitted in any form or by any means, electronic or mechanical, including photocopying and recording, or by any information storage and retrieval system, except in the case of brief quotations for use in articles and reviews, without written permission from the author.

Scripture quotations are from the NIV (New International Version), Copyright 1973, 1978, 1984, International Bible Society unless otherwise noted.

The views expressed in this book are the author's and do not necessarily reflect those of the publisher.

www.WorldwidePublishingGroup.com
7710-T Cherry Park Dr, Ste 224
Houston, Texas 77095
(713) 766-4271

Additional Resources

www.holyfirebooks.com

As you read this book, keep the theme in mind, which is to know **WHO** you are, as well as **WHOSE** you are.

Recognize your identity, your sonship or "daughtership" in Christ, your eternal relationship with Abba (Father) God through His Son Jesus Christ, by the power of the Holy Spirit!

Contents

Dedication ix
Foreword xi
A Personal Note From The Author xiii
Acknowledgments xv
Introduction... xix
Part 1: Relationship Collisions... 1
Chapter 1: Where Did Blind Spots Originate? 3
Part 2: Blind Spots That Hinder Relationships 11
Chapter 2: Shame... 13
Chapter 3: Guilt.. 21
Chapter 4: Fear... 27
Chapter 5: Anxiety & Worry 43
Chapter 6: Offense.. 53
Part 3: Blind Spots That Can Manipulate Relationships ... 63
Chapter 7: Transference.. 65
Chapter 8: Foolishness.. 71
Chapter 9: Pride & Rebellion.. 77
Part 4: Blind Spots That Can Destroy Relationships 89
Chapter 10: Arrogance 911
Chapter 11: Anger & Control... 99
Chapter 12: Temptation 107
Chapter 13: Lust... 113
Chapter 14: Addiction 125
Chapter 15: Ministry 131
Chapter 16: Deception 145

Chapter 17: Unforgiveness 155
Epilogue 167
Appendix: Process of Identity 169
Testimonials 173
About the Author 185

Dedication

I dedicate this book to my beautiful wife, helpmate, and best friend of over 22 years, Karen Ann Baxter. Karen understood God's call on my life as she later in our marriage sacrificed almost ten years not being near our daughter, son-in-law, or our grandchildren that live in Texas. Karen married me and came on this life journey knowing that I love, trust, and try my best to follow Jesus in all I do.

Before our marriage in June of 1997, but mostly after we married, Karen began to see God's call on my life to follow Jesus roll out as I evangelized, healed the sick, preached and taught God's word.

Karen also experienced part of the call on my life including over seven years of school, which led me to my Master of Ministry degree (M.Min.). After being ordained as a pastor in August 2007—with my wife by my side—I planted my first church, Ramona Vineyard Church, in October 2012 in Ramona, California. We ended the season at Ramona Vineyard Church as I obeyed God, by shutting down the church, not handing off the baton and moved to Conroe, Texas in October 2016. Karen was pleased, as she now would be near our daughter, son-in-law, and our four grandchildren.

On February 6, 2017, God spoke to me about writing this book, my first book, *Discover Your Blind Spots*. Once again, my encouraging, patient, totally supportive, beautiful wife stood by my side as I spent long hours compiling and writing this book.

Karen, thank you for standing by my side and trusting that I heard correctly through the Holy Spirit for our present and near plans, encouraging me along the way, even when things got hard during the church plant, and then shutting down the church, and then again being patient as I wrote this book.

Foreword

God created us to exist in the context of community; we are not meant to live in isolation. I'm convinced that one of the reasons God created mankind was, that we need each other to help us to see our blind spots. A blind spot is something that requires our attention, but we cannot see it. We need God to reveal it to us or, as He often does, use someone to bring it to our attention. Blind spots hinder us from becoming and achieving that which God intends for us. They create problems in our relationships with one another and with God. Blind spots rob of us of our inheritance, our identity and ultimately our destiny. We need to be able to see our blind spots. Thus, we need one another to help us know and understand what we are blind to, and we need those that will do it with courage, boldness, grace, love, compassion, and mercy.

I have known Pastor Mark Baxter for several years. He is a beloved friend and a gifted pastor, teacher, and evangelist. He truly cares for the people God called him to shepherd, and he has a heart for the lost. You will feel that care in the way he approaches this book because he approaches it not just as a teaching, but also as a pastor ministering to his sheep. In his education, Mark simplifies potentially complex issues, and he does that in this book as he "unpacks" the various blind spots, which can be present in our lives. However, Mark is also careful not to assume that a book can accomplish everything needed to deal with blind spots, particularly those that are more deeply entrenched and those caused by severe woundedness. He wisely directs you, the reader, to Biblically grounded, competent, and compassionate counselors, pastors, and communities of believers. These are the people who can facilitate, and the context in which, deliverance and healing from blind spots are most likely to occur.

This book serves as a great launching point for becoming aware of what blind spots can exist in our life, and by bringing that awareness, can potentially give rise to a revelation by the Spirit as to which ones may be present. We can then seek the people, and the help we need to be set free and experience the wholeness through Christ that we deserve. We are meant to live victorious and joy-filled lives in the context of loving and united communities who serve Him wholeheartedly. So, get ready to see what you haven't been able to see – those blind spots which have hindered your walk with God and your relationships with others. Are you ready to receive the upgrade He has for you?

-- **Jim Kubiak,** Equipping Minister

Harvest Valley Worship Center, Sandpoint, Idaho

A Personal Note From The Author

Reading my book isn't the fix-all method! That, my new friend, is not my job! I wholeheartedly believe it is God's job, through Jesus, and the power of the Holy Spirit, to show you what you need.

If you are a follower of Jesus, please take a moment and ask the Lord to give you Holy Spirit lenses to see clear as you read, ponder, and pray through the writing of this book.

Pause here and ask Father God this question: "How is my vertical relationship with you?" Until that is in focus, it will be complicated to navigate your horizontal relationships to understand the collateral damage caused by the actions of your Blind Spots.

My hope and prayers are this; by the time you finish this book that the person of the Holy Spirit will highlight one or more of your Blind Spots.

My number one purpose in this book is for you to begin to see through God's Word and these life stories to take steps to discover the damage done by the Blind Spots(s) in your own life.

Secondly, I'm hoping you will have the opportunity to deal with and dissolve the damage that you have caused in your own life along with open doors to help restore some of your broken past or present relationships, but *only* if no further emotional or physical harm is to come to you or them.

Thirdly, I hope as you deal with your Blind Spots(s), that this book lovingly helps you to point out a Blind Spots(s) to your friends and/or family, which in turn will help them to walk through and restore some of their broken relationships with others.

If you aren't a follower of Jesus but are tired of steering your own life, then give the steering wheel of your life to Jesus today by reading this simple prayer aloud. Jesus, I realize I'm a sinner, and I'm in need of a savior; please forgive my sins that you died on the cross for, please come into my heart and dwell forever as you change me from the inside out to be more like you. This day I give up my steering wheel of life to you! Amen. If you just said this prayer, then let me congratulate you! If you have Christian friends, let them know right away and get plugged into a local church body so you can further your growth in your new faith walk with Jesus. If you don't currently have a Christian friend, please seek out a local Bible-believing church to get plugged in.

Relationships begin the moment one loving word is spoken to the one we are praying for or one touch as they experience the presence of God invading their personal space.

It is the reason why, "I call Father God, 'the Loving Ambusher,' because he sneaks up and loves on those he has created."

-- Pastor Mark Baxter

I hope you find this read both enjoyable and rewarding!

Acknowledgments

I would like to thank my mom and dad for always being there, even though they weren't Christians at the time; they were still very supportive in all my endeavors. My mom and both of my sisters will have the opportunity to read this book.

However, it saddens me that my dad and my brother Barry will not be able to read my book. Barry, 42-years-old, was killed in a head-on collision and went home to be with Jesus in 1998. "In 2009, my dad came to Christ at 79 years of age. Then on October 11th, 2010, after a year-long battle with lung cancer, he went to be with Jesus."

As far as I know, I'm the only pastor in our family history on both my dad and mom's side. The morning after I performed my dad's celebration of life, I had the great privilege to lead my mom, my older sister Pamela Baxter and younger sister Denise Baxter to faith in Christ.

I would like to thank the late Dr. Bill Jackson (Jax) who was a best friend, a Vineyard pastor for over 35 years, an incredible academic, and curriculum writer along with being the Author of "The Quest for the Radical Middle," and his life work "NOTHINSGONNASTOPIT." Jax went home to be with Jesus in June 2015. I'm proud to say that he was my professor for seven and a half years. I will never forget him telling me that my first Master's paper turned into him was like reading a book and not at all like academic writing. He went on to say that he would eventually make me just as good of an academic writer as I was a preacher. If he were still with us, he most certainly would've been the principal editor of this book and would have written the foreword in this book. Bill Jackson was an incredible professor that cared more about his students' growth in following Jesus than focusing on the grades themselves. Along with being a great friend, he was the most personable professor I've ever had along with Travis Twyman, Senior Pastor of Inland Vineyard Church in Corona, California, running a close second.

I would like to thank Bruce Henderson, a friend, and also a Vineyard pastor for over 35 years, who on several occasions gave me a prophetic word that I would be writing books. The first time I received a prophetic word from Bruce was at a pastors/leadership conference at Vineyard Church of Anaheim in California. It was shortly after the Witch Creek Fire, which in its destructive path took my wife's and my home in Ramona, California. The second time a word came through Bruce for me on writing books was years later at Dwell Vineyard in La Mesa, CA. as Bruce taught a conference on "Hearing Gods Voice."

I would like to thank my friend, Pastor Jim Kubiak, of Ramona, California. Jim's prophetic word on me writing books was spoken one night at a once-a-month all-community worship night called "Revive Ramona." The venue for the monthly meeting was at Ramona Vineyard Church, where I was the Senior Pastor. Within seconds after Jim delivered his prophetic word to me, it was confirmed through pastor Bill Burkhardt, of Life Gate Community Church. Bill, whom I did not know previously, was the guest speaker that night. He began by piggybacking off Jim's word as he continued to speak more confirmation about certain things I had been praying about for many years. He continued to prophesy that God was going to start answering certain prayers, and the last part of his prophetic word was, "Ramona Vineyard Church was just a tiny part of God's plan for me and not to ever despise the smaller things as bigger things were coming my way."

I would like to thank Jay West, Author of the books, *Kingdom Encounters*, Downloads *From Heaven, Willing To Yield*, and *Well, Well, Well*. His ministry includes ANOINTED 2 GO MdM, a Multi-

Denominational Ministry, and Pastor/planter of Kingdom Encounters Church in Omaha, Nebraska, along with being a Nebraska representative for the US prayer council. I met Jay through doing ministry with Pastor Bill Jackson and Todd Volker in the Inland Empire in California many years ago. I called Jay one day to touch base with him and let him know I was approaching the point of writing my first book.

Last, but not least, a special thanks to the beautiful people of *Ramona Vineyard Church*, who I had the incredible privilege to serve four wonderful years, from October 2012 to October 2016.

Encourager's for the community of *Ramona Vineyard Church*: Cheri McKnight, Dan Moreno, Linda Kinkaid, Rachel Scanlan.

Annabelle Andrews and Leon Andrews (board member), key leaders

Cindy Hasz: board member, women's director, prayer team member, and intercessor.

Erin Williams: worship leader, singer and prayer warrior.

Hannah Fuentes: worship leader and singer.

Katrina Myhre: prayer team member

Lorrena McCoy: prayer team member and intercessor.

Marylin Boecher: prayer team member and intercessor.

Robert Gonzales, board member, and a key leader.

Roy Tovar (board member) and Cathy Tovar key leaders.

Scott Lacey: worship team guitarist and singer.

Introduction

Just as each vehicle you and I purchase have blind spots, we as humans have them as well. If you are willing to be humble and open to change in your own life, God will reveal your Blind Spots just as he has and continues to show mine to me. When I finally opened up to God to trust him, I began to recognize that not only did he truly love me, but that he cared about every single little or big detail in my life. It was at that time the Lord gently began showing me my Blind Spots as He pointed out my somewhat skewed relationship with Him, and how that affected every single one of my past, and present relationships.

After you begin the process of embracing your Blind Spots(s), *you will be able to see more clearly,* and take inventory of the damage you have done as you accept responsibility for your wrong actions. Am I the only one who sees this? Or do you also find it strange, that we always seem to hurt the ones closest to us? After all, we aren't going to walk down the street to see a perfect stranger and begin pointing the finger and yelling at them. Our lives are no different when we act out our Blind Spot(s), as we cause damaged relationships that are minor, major, and even sometimes so broken that they become irreparable.

Two questions to ponder:

- Do you see the Blind Spots in your life?
- Why do you think people don't see their Blind Spots?

Because they are just that, they are Blind Spots!

My hope and prayers are that this book full of Scripture, biblical stories, and real-life personal stories will give you some information along with some tools to help you discover, admit, and deal with any Blind Spots in your present journey of life.

Father God, I pray that as my new friend reads this book, that through each chapter you will gently reveal every Blind Spot(s) in their life as you have and continue in mine through the Holy Spirit and people too.

Father, as you reveal and peel back the layers of damage that a Blind Spot(s) has caused, that each person reading this book will find some resolve, that will lead to reconciliation, along with deep healing for them in the present, and past damaged, and broken relationships. Father, I ask that also you will reveal where some relationships have been hurtful by going back to try to rebuild them in person, and that each person can, from a distance, forgive, and reconcile peace with and through you. –In Jesus' name, Amen

Enjoy the rest of the journey as you keep your heart open so that your Blind Spot(s) will come forth.

Part 1
Relationship Collisions

Chapter 1
Where Did Blind Spots Originate?

NO ONE IS IMMUNE TO BLIND SPOTS!

We are all naive to our Blind Spots that will remain hidden until God or someone who knows us and loves us points them out.

Whether you are a religious person, against religion, agnostic, atheist or a follower of Christ, you can expect to have relational collisions one day.

The question here is what you will do when relational collisions do happen in your life? In other words, what lengths will you go to get your resolve? Will you turn to something to block the relevant emotional feelings, such as the use of alcohol, other drugs, food, or pornography, etc?

What can cause these relational collisions? Blind Spots!

So once again, the same two questions that I asked in my introductory chapter,

- Do you see the Blind Spots in your life?
- Why do you think people don't see their Blind Spots?

Because they are just that, they are Blind Spots!

Where would you say Blind Spots originated?

Since the year I preached and taught at Ramona Vineyard Church on this 12-week mini-series, I have had the opportunity to ask literally hundreds of Christians, including pastors, and lay workers, this same question.

Think about how you would answer this next question?

Everyone I have asked this question seems to come up with the same answer, which is this, Blind Spots started in the Garden of Eden when the serpent tempted Eve with the fruit in Genesis 3:1-6.

If this was your answer too, I hate to burst your bubble, but that answer is incorrect. However, Scripture does give us a clue, so please take a moment to pause and read this passage:

> *For God knows that when you eat from it your eyes will be opened, and you will be like God, knowing good and evil* (Genesis 3:5).

Did the clue give you the total answer?

NO! But it does give a hint of the answer.

Part of the answer is in the narrative in the book of *Isaiah*, and the other part finishes off in the book of *Revelation*.

To be able to get a more unobstructed view of this book, please pause here and read these two short passages below. You will see the picture of how Lucifer/Satan wanted to be equal to God!

> *How you have fallen from heaven,*
>
> *morning star, son of the dawn!*
>
> *You have been cast down to the earth,*
>
> *you who once laid low the nations!*
>
> *13 You said in your heart,*
>
> *"I will ascend to the heavens;*

I will raise my throne

above the stars of God;

I will sit enthroned on the mount of assembly,

on the utmost heights of Mount Zaphon.

14 *I will ascend above the tops of the clouds;*

I will make myself like the Most High."

15 *But you are brought down to the realm of the dead, to the depths of the pit* (Isaiah 14:12-15).

Then war broke out in heaven. Michael and his angels fought against the dragon, and the dragon and his angels

fought back. 8 *But he was not strong enough, and they lost their place in heaven.*

9 *The great dragon was hurled down—that ancient serpent called the devil, or Satan, who leads the whole world astray.*

He was hurled to the earth, and his angels with him.

10 *Then I heard a loud voice in heaven say:*

"Now have come the salvation and the power

and the kingdom of our God,

and the authority of his Messiah.

For the accuser of our brothers and sisters,

who accuses them before our God day and night,

has been hurled down.

11 *They triumphed over him*

> *by the blood of the Lamb*
> *and by the word of their testimony;*
> *they did not love their lives so much*
> *as to shrink from death.*
> *12 Therefore rejoice, you heavens*
> *and you who dwell in them!*
> *But woe to the earth and the sea,*
> *because the devil has gone down to you!*
> *He is filled with fury, because he knows that his time is short"*
>
> (Revelation 12:7-12).

So, now we see that Blind Spots originated when Satan wanted to be like God! Now that you have that view of the origin of Blind Spots, you can begin the journey through this book.

What is a blind spot?

A blind spot is a portion of a field that cannot be seen or inspected with available equipment.

A blind spot can be a subject that you do not understand well, often because you do not want to know or admit the truth about it.

Here is a spiritual definition of Blind Spot:

As a pastor, I see it as a form of punishment Satan orchestrates to keep people believing that God doesn't care what happens to them, and the ones they love.

Over the years, I have witnessed many relational collisions. Some collisions are minor, some are moderate, and still, others have caused major catastrophes in peoples' lives.

If these relational collisions continue, they can cause long-lasting problems in your current relationships. They can also add future damage for many years in new relationships resulting in more emotional hurt for others, as wells as you too. A fact of life is:

Hurting People Hurt People!

Some of these relational collisions happen to pastors, more of fleshing that out in coming chapters in this book.

As I watch all the devastation in the United States, and around the world, my thoughts immediately take me back to a Pharisee that lived in the 1st century named Saul. Saul had Blind Spots revealed in his relational collision with God on the road to Damascus. Saul found himself knocked to the ground and blinded on the road to Damascus. As a young Pharisee, Saul was headed to Damascus to gain more recognition as a persecutor of those in a sect called the "Way." This was before they were called Christians in the book of Acts.

> *Then Barnabas went to Tarsus to look for Saul, 26 and when he found him, he brought him to Antioch. So, for a whole year Barnabas and Saul met with the church and taught great numbers of people. The disciples were called Christians first at Antioch (Acts 11:25-26).*

> *Meanwhile, Saul was still breathing out murderous threats against the Lord's disciples. He went to the high priest 2 and asked him for letters to the synagogues in Damascus, so that if he found any there who belonged to the Way, whether men or women, he might take them as prisoners to Jerusalem. 3 As he neared Damascus on his journey, suddenly a light from heaven flashed around him. 4*

> *He fell to the ground and heard a voice say to him, "Saul, Saul, why do you persecute me?" 5 "Who are you, Lord?" Saul asked. "I am Jesus, whom you are persecuting," he replied. 6 "Now get up and go into the city, and you will be told what you must do* (Acts 9:1-6).

Saul had a Blind Spot of Arrogance, as well as a Blind Spot of Pride before his conversion to Christ. He saw the cross as a form of punishment, and an example to families not to break the Roman law. The cross in Saul's eyes would have been a symbol of shame for the families related to that person crucified. As a Pharisee, Saul would have viewed the cross as a victory for the Pious religious sect.

Even though Saul studied the Old Testament Scriptures, and assumed he knew everything about Yahweh—what Yahweh's plans were for life, in general, but more importantly for eternal life—he still somehow missed the truth of the Messiah in the Scriptures. Even in the book of *Isaiah*, Saul didn't seem to see it. However, when Saul got saved/received eternal life through his encounter with Jesus on the road to Damascus, he then went from his Hebrew name, *Saul*; and took on his Greek name, *Paul*.

Paul learned what it was like for those he had previously pursued prior to his conversion, as he too endured persecution. He suffered trials, imprisonment, suffering, and sorrow as he lived out the truth of the One who hung on the cross—i.e., Jesus Christ.

Saul had a Blind Spot of Arrogance as well as a Blind Spot of Pride, but after he encountered Jesus on the road to Damascus, he as Paul was healed of his Blind Spots as he now saw the cross as a victory!

The Apostle Paul Came to Realize…

- Paul learned that God loves us with unconditional love no matter what we have done in the past, present, or what we will do in the future. We can't make God love us more, and he will never love us less.

"Come now, let us settle the matter," says the Lord "Though your sins are like scarlet, they shall be as white as snow; though they are red as crimson, they shall be like wool. 19 If you are willing and obedient, you will eat the good things of the land (Isaiah 1:18-19).

- In Saul's conversion to the Apostle Paul, he learned that we are all invited to have a personal relationship with the one true God. That same God, was the God of all creation, and the One who knows all, and is in all.

    Through him all things were made; without him nothing was made that has been made (John 1:3).

- Paul learned that God sent his Son, Jesus, to give mercy and grace that he did not deserve. It was the second person of the Trinity, Jesus Christ himself, who hung on the cross to take the sting of death away and give him eternal life.

    Where, O death, is your victory? Where, O death, is your sting?" 56 The sting of death is sin, and the power of sin is the law. 57 But thanks be to God! He gives us the victory through our Lord Jesus Christ (1 Corinthians 15:55-57).

But God demonstrates his own love for us in this: While we were still sinners, Christ died for us (Romans 5:8)

Broken People Cause More Breakage and More Emotional Hurt

Don't wait for a relational collision(s) to deal with your Blind Spot(s)!

As you journey through the next 16 chapters, I hope you will be awakened to your Blind Spot(s) to prevent any further relational collisions in your journey of life!

Part 2

Blind Spots That Hinder Relationships

Chapter 2
Shame

When I was a young man growing up in Washington State, my mom's mom, my grandma Hilda Hinkley, would sometimes babysit my three siblings, and me. I remember one of my least fond memories of my grandma coming to help my mom while my dad was in Korea in the army.

My older brother Barry and I used to love to go on outdoor adventures and pretend to camp. One rainy day while pretending that we were camping in the living room, I had a great idea. I took both of our plastic toy army canteens and filled them with water at the kitchen sink.

As I finished filling the canteens, my grandma entered the kitchen. As she saw me leaving the kitchen, she called me back into the kitchen and immediately asked if there was any water in the canteens. I didn't want to say "yes," but I didn't want to lie either. However, I chose the latter, and I lied to her as my face felt like it was on fire, as I tried to pull the wool over my grandma's eyes, which I knew would be an impossible task.

My grandma being wise said to me, please open one of the canteens and turn it upside down. So, as my face color turned to what must have looked like second-degree sunburn or like the hot coals in my dad's barbecue, I slowly opened one of the canteens and turned it upside down as the water poured onto the kitchen floor. As if I wasn't already embarrassed enough and feeling shame, my grandma called my brother into the kitchen, and tossed us both dishtowels, and told us to clean up the water, and then for us both to head to our bedrooms for the day to think about the lie I had told her.

What is shame?

Shame is a painful feeling of humiliation or distress caused by the consciousness of wrong or foolish behavior done to self or by others.

After Eve ate the forbidden fruit from the tree and then handed it to her husband Adam, their spiritual eyes were open wide as they both now saw they were nude.

> *Then the eyes of both of them were opened, and they realized they were naked; so they sewed fig leaves together and made coverings for themselves* (Genesis 3:7).

Shame is something that sometimes can be resolved quickly through prayer and counseling. However, when it becomes a Blind Spot of Shame, it is that type of deep shame that can be paralyzing and cause the one who feels it to cover it up. Adam and Eve did this with fig leaves.

Fig leaves are indeed harmless, but it isn't those safe fig leaves we see people using to cover the Blind Spot of Shame. Instead, we see boys, girls, men, and women that tend to use alcohol or other drugs along with food, or sometimes enter destructive sexual relations as a cover-up for the shame.

The Shame that I'm talking about here is like a full body tattoo that Satan imprints on someone. As a result, the person that carries the shame feels as if they are like a walking billboard for the world to see. Even though others can't visually see shame, it can be so deep emotionally that the person carrying it feels like everyone does see it and judges him or her for it.

We can't see the wind, but we can look at the effects of the wind such as a leaf blowing in a tree. A leaf blowing in a tree is harmless and can be pleasurable to the eye. However, when I moved to Texas in 2016, I soon found out there are times when the wind takes on a more drastic personality, like a tornado or hurricane leaving paths of destruction.

Even though the naked eye can't visually see the shame, still others can see what the effects of it are through behavioral patterns in a person's life.

Something that is overlooked and hidden in all societies, is the adult man, that takes advantage of young adult naïve women virgins to brag to their buddies about their sexual encounters. Sad enough to say, as a man in my destructive years, this was my mindset. This type of behavior ends up bringing shame to the women that become trophies. The emotional damage can cause some women to distrust all men, sometimes to turn to an alternative lifestyle or maybe not ever to enter marriage with a man, and if they do marry, they often become standoffish sexually with their husbands until they receive deep emotional healing.

Many are sinned against by people outside the family circle— e.g., community rapist or physical abusers. However, boys, girls, men, and women are shameful by the actions others have done to them by so-called trustworthy relatives or so-called close family friends. Especially is the case with minor children who are targeted daily by predators living in darkness as part of the family or within a circle of friends.

One of my incredible and caring professors while in Masters, Dr. Leah Coulter, says that those sinned against need a voice for the injustice done to them, whether it is molestation and emotional or physical abuse. In a nutshell, Dr. Leah Coulter would say, "The person sinned against needs to put the sin that was committed against them in the courtroom of God's heart." (paraphrase) In other words, forgive the one who sinned, and allow God to deal with them. In so doing, you can remain free from an emotional connection with the offender. (See Unforgiveness in Chapter 15.)

Please hear this loud and clear!

Forgiving an action does not right the wrong done!

Forgiving an action does not right the wrong done!

Forgiving an action does not right the wrong done!

What forgiveness does, is it brings freedom to the person sinned against and can open the door to get rid of the Shame feeling. When we refuse to forgive an offense, we are connected so-to-speak to the person that committed the offense/sin against us.

As a pastor for years, I have heard this statement: you don't know what I have endured! And in many cases, I didn't realize the extent of the damage they suffered. However, when they shared their life hurts with me, I could then empathize with them as I walked out the journey of healing with the ones that were willing.

If we pause and begin to think of these three things below, it makes more sense to forgive!

- We were created to be at peace in both our mind and body. When we refuse to forgive, it is an un-peaceful feeling and is like a foreign object that needs to exit out of the body. Refusing to forgive can be a Blind Spot that causes a constant battle of tension in mind, and body until it is surrendered, and released as it finally exits the body and mind. It is after this, that the lousy emotion is gone.
- Why would we want to rent/lease space out in our mind to continually think about someone who has harmed us?
- The emotional stress is as if we are carrying the offender's physical weight on us daily and if more than one offender the weight factor compounds.

Now that the Blind Spot of Shame has revealed its ugly head, hopefully, you will be able to exit the little v status (victim) and move to the big V status, Victor!

Questions to ponder and room to write as you leave this chapter!

How was this chapter helpful in my current circumstances?

_____
_____
_____
_____

Why am I feeling Shame in my life?

_____
_____
_____
_____

What are some of the behavioral patterns of the Shame I still carry?

_____
_____
_____
_____

What is the depth of innocence in my Shame?

_____
_____
_____
_____

What are my next steps to move towards freedom from my Shame?

_____

_____

_____

_____

God invites us to come to Him 24/7 with any of our life issues. He knows our pain and wants to hear our voices, so He can heal us emotionally, physically, and spiritually!

Before entering the next chapter on Guilt, please pause and pray this prayer:

Father God, thank you for highlighting and revealing my Blind Spot of Shame. Help me to focus on how good You are, and how much You truly love and care for me no matter what I have done or what's been done to me.

Lord, as I continue to walk out my journey in healing with you, help me to read your Word as you open the door to take the proper steps to dissolve the damage done to my relationships. As I release all of the stuff on my mind right now, I give it to you God, and I receive your peace.

> *And the peace of God, which transcends all understanding, will guard your hearts and your minds in Christ Jesus* (Philippians 4:7).

Thank you, Holy Spirit for replacing those Shameful thoughts with your words of truth. You know what concerns me! I choose this day to guard my heart and not to allow shame to control my life as I focus my mind on what truth is in the midst of turmoil I may face because I know you go before me and you have my back.

Father God, I realize just reading this book is not enough for total healing, so I pray that you will place the right pastors, leaders, counselors, and friends who understand me to walk the rest of this healing journey with me.

I pray these things in Jesus name! Amen.

I pray as you seek God that he will not only heal your past or present Shame, but he will help you in your current walk and journey with Him as you head into the future. Remember—God is always pursuing a deeper and more intimate relationship with you.

Your new friend,

Pastor Mark

Chapter 3
Guilt

Six-year-old Jerry had so much guilt that he wasn't able to face his father when he came home from work. His father had told him numerous times never to enter the garage while he was away from home. Jerry went into the garage to look for his slingshot that he wasn't supposed to play with unsupervised. When he saw it on the top shelf, he proceeded to climb to retrieve it. In doing so, Jerry knocked down a 1937 Ford bumper that landed and cracked the middle of the windshield of the 1937 Ford truck his father was restoring.

What is guilt?

Guilt is a feeling of responsibility or remorse for some offense, crime, wrong, etc., whether real or imagined.

Guilt is that dreadful feeling that causes our stomach to toss and turn when we know we have done wrong, and we'll go to almost any extreme to rid ourselves of it unless it is a Blind Spot of Guilt.

Guilt and shame sometimes go hand in hand, and the same action may give rise to feelings of both shame and guilt. The former reflects how we feel about ourselves, and the latter involves an awareness that our wrong actions have injured ourselves, or someone else emotionally, and or physically.

Adam and Eve established a human pattern that continues to this day. First comes the cover-up, and then we play the blame game as we try to justify or rationalize our actions. We tend to believe that the more we can blame someone else, the less guilty we will feel. Both shame and guilt were birthed in the Garden of Eden and were fully orchestrated by the serpent with the temptation of the forbidden fruit to Eve, and to her husband, Adam.

Some will try to escape from guilt through activities, alcohol, or drugs, etc. Or we run to psychiatrists, but it is secular psychiatry that has attempted to solve the problem of guilt by saying there is no such thing as sin. Psychiatry would tell us to ignore the guilty feeling because it is baseless. We try, but somehow, we can't pull it off. Why not?

We can't escape these feelings by ignoring them because God built into our human knowledge of right and wrong a moral code. God's Word speaks of the moral conscience, which exists even within those who are not aware of His laws.

One example of this in *Romans* 2:14-15, ESV:

> *For when Gentiles, who do not have the law, by nature do what the law requires, they are a law to themselves, even though they do not have the law. 15 They show that the work of the law is written on their hearts, while their conscience also bears witness, and their conflicting thoughts accuse or even excuse them.*

Some people's shame can be so great that feelings of guilt are restricted. That is, until something happens to spark that thought to guide them first to remorse, and then to the path of confession and repentance. (See Shame in Chapter 2.)

After the movie "The Passion of the Christ" came to the theatres, a man by the name of Dan Leach went to see the film. During his watching of the movie, he could no longer live with the guilt of the murder he had committed six weeks beforehand. Dan murdered his girlfriend that he believed was pregnant. However, it wasn't until Dan saw Christ flogged as a public shame, and then being crucified as an innocent man, that his Blind Spot of Guilt had shown, and he went the police department to confess to the murder of his girlfriend. Previously, he had orchestrated the murder to look like a suicide.

> *If we confess our sins, he is faithful and just and will forgive us our sins and purify us from all unrighteousness* (1 John 1:9).

Another example of a Blind Spot of Guilt might be a person(s) that every time they are around something that goes wrong, they would feel as if they were somehow partially or fully guilty of it happening.

Blind Spots of Guilt can also derive from different circumstances in one's life such as these following examples:

- Being molested or physically beaten or abused as a minor and being told that it was their fault it was happening.
- When parents divorce, children tend to blame themselves, which causes guilt. Let's face it; every single person will deal with guilt in his or her lifetime.

> *For God did not send his Son into the world to condemn the world, but to save the world through him* (John 3:17).

Guilt Is Only Good If It Keeps You From Repeating The Same Offense!

> *Therefore, there is now no condemnation for those who are in Christ Jesus* (Romans 8:1).

Questions to ponder and room to write as you leave this chapter!

How was this chapter helpful in my current circumstances?

_____
_____
_____
_____

What have I done to create my feeling of Guilt?

_____
_____
_____
_____

Who have I hurt in my path of Guilt?

_____
_____
_____
_____

What are my next steps to move towards freedom from my Guilt?

_____
_____
_____
_____

Before entering the next chapter on Fear, please pause and pray this prayer:

Father God, thank you for highlighting and revealing my Blind Spot of Guilt.

Holy Spirit, as I continue this healing journey with you, convict me when I'm about to do something that will bring on more guilt in my life.

Thank you, Father God, for showing me that Your Word can not only show me how guilt is birthed, but also can give me passages of Scripture to receive healing from guilt.

Lord, I receive your rest today, as I remember that You want to solve my life issues. I embrace the thought of you healing my relationships and me!

Heavenly Father, I realize just reading this book is not enough for total healing, so I pray that you will place the right pastors, leaders, counselors, and friends who understand me to walk the rest of this healing journey with me.

I pray these things in Jesus name! Amen.

I realize that some of these stories and scripture might hit a raw spot in your mind or heart about Guilt, so I pray as you seek God that he will not only heal your Guilt of past and present, but He will also show you how to avoid Guilt in the future.

Remember, God is always pursuing a deeper and more intimate relationship with you.

Your new friend,

Pastor Mark

Chapter 4
Fear

*"Many of our fears are tissue-paper-thin, and a
single courageous step would carry us
clear through them."*
-- Brendan Francis

What is fear?

Fear is an unpleasant emotion caused by the belief that someone or something is dangerous, likely to cause pain or a threat.

As a pastor, I have learned that God will call us to lean into and embrace fear to find the faith to pray through it and experience a breakthrough.

What fears limit you from moving forward in life?

- Fear of death?
- Fear of life?
- Fear of success?
- Fear of failure?
- Fear of not fitting in?
- Fear of Man?
- Fear of poverty?
- Fear of decisions?

If regret and anxiety from a past relationship now threaten any future relationships, we must find peace for the present. If left unchecked, fear can become so unmanageable that it will become a Blind Spot.

The strongholds in our hearts and minds can keep us prisoners of fear. They can also be rooted in bitterness, which produces destructive emotions, and actions that cause further relational collisions developing a Blind Spot of Fear.

When you know who you are in Christ, fear can become a simple acronym, False Evidence Appearing Real. But what about those people that are always afraid, and don't recognize that in reality, it is a Blind Spot of Fear.

One of Satan's most popular and powerful weapons that he uses against us is Fear. Sometimes it can overwhelm us with a thick shadow of darkness, which controls our every move, confusing the decisions we have to make day-to-day! If we are living under the weight of the "what if's" in life, it can cause fear which becomes a hard place to dwell and can become a Blind Spot.

There is a lot of craziness around all of us today! Like wars, conflicts, persecution, violence, crime, natural disasters, terrorism, unemployment, disease, and death to name a few. People fear for their children's future, their family's safety, along with the fear of financial stability. The list goes on and on and on, but there is a lot we could potentially fear.

Many people equate the word intimacy with sex. You can have sex with no intimacy, and you can have intimacy with no sex, and then you can have sex, and intimacy at the same time.

However, a fear that is more common than people realize is the fear of intimacy.

INTIMACY------or-------- INTO – ME - SEE

In other words, you are afraid to allow God, a family member, a spouse, co-worker, or someone else to look inside you deeper.

Some people are afraid to open up to others in fear that the other person won't like them when they find out who they are.

Because of this Blind Spot of Fear, they think if someone gets to know them, they can't or won't love them. It's a massive lie from the evil one!

This group of people generally avoids what they see as a preventive hurt, by running away first to prevent someone getting to know them at all.

What about abandonment issues that lead to a Blind Spot of Fear?

Abandonment issues can be like a double-sided coin:

One side of the coin is:

- When you live somewhere for a long time, have lots of friends, and family around, and some job opportunity takes you to a different city or state. Now, those you were closest to, depended on for friendship, trusted for advice, become missing pieces in your life.

The other side of the coin is:

- When your childhood friends you have been around for many years decide to move far away.

  Later, in adulthood, it becomes much deeper, causing real hurtful emotional scars, which might stem from those childhood memories of abandonment.

This next story has to do with abandonment issues that led to a Blind Spot of Fear. Before you read it, I want you to know that *abandonment issues can connect to almost every chapter in this book.*

I spent my younger years with my mom and dad, my sisters Pam and Denise, and my brother Barry in Quincy, Yakima, and Ellensburg, Washington.

I remember when we lived in Ellensburg. My older sister Pam graduated high school and joined the army. My younger sister Denise seemed out of sorts for a while. Pam, and Denise at a very young age played together as siblings do and hung out with each other on a regular basis. However, Pam—being five years older than Denise—had a much older circle of friends. Even though, Denise had her own younger circle of friends, I would notice when Pam was with her friends at our home that Denise felt left out!

- In 1971, we took a family vacation to California to visit my grandpa and grandma Burke, my Uncle Bill and Aunt Bernice, and their family. When we returned from vacation, my dad and mom decided to make a new start and move our family to California. At first, the news seemed exciting, and welcoming until it sunk in, that we would be leaving all our immediate neighborhood friends, extended local friends, classmates, and especially our extended family behind.

- As I look back now, I can see how devastating the move turned out for Denise, more so than me. I was, and still am extroverted, as my sister Denise leans more towards introverted.

- We made the enormous move to California during the summer of 1972, when I was 15-years old. In 1973, my brother, just like my older sister Pam, graduated high school, and joined the army. I forgot to mention, that my dad was a career army guy of 20 years, so they followed in his footsteps.

- I am outgoing, so I met a lot of new friends in the mobile home park we moved into. Denise met friends in the park too, as most of my friends in the park had younger brothers, and sisters that became her friends.

- I met more friends in high school and started hanging out with them on a regular basis away from the mobile home park. This meant that once again, without me realizing it, Denise might have felt a sense of abandonment, first by Pam, then Barry, and now by me, too.

Now, let me fast forward! Denise entered her senior year of high school during the summer of 1975, and within a month of me graduating high school, I moved to Woodlake, California, 315 miles away.

I had been so busy with my own life; I didn't even consider how abandoned Denise might have felt, and the fear that could have set in, as she was the only sibling left at home with my parents.

- I didn't think to even ask her how she was feeling about me leaving, although she did more than once say, that she was going to miss me, as she saw me packing to move.

- As I look back now, I can remember the weeks leading up to my departure, and right down to the days before I left, Denise wasn't around much.

- Even though, I was always so busy with my friends, and not home a whole lot, I still at that time was living in the same home with Denise, and my mom and dad.

- I regret me being so busy about me, as I never considered that Denise might be hiding some form of depression, or loneliness; knowing I would no longer be there at night to laugh with her, watch shows, play cards, or have a simple conversation.

- My sister Denise, at 60 years old has never married, currently lives with my 90-year-old mother in her home in Washington State, and they are best friends. My sister Pam lives in California with her son, and his family in an adjoining granny flat on their home. My brother Barry was hit by a concrete truck and killed in a head-on collision. My dad died of cancer in October of 2010. So, as you can see, our family still living, is scattered in three different states.

- Some people tend to believe that since the family is now far away, and the old friends are no longer available to fellowship with, or confide in, that the new set of friends someday will also abandon them. They might even tend to feel the same way towards God.

Before publishing this book, I called my sister Denise to ask her permission to publish a personal story concerning her. I read my story to her on my cellphone and received her permission. Denise immediately said it all made sense, as she could see how the abandonment issues growing up could easily have led to a Blind Spot of Fear in her life.

If you related to Denise's story, you might also have a Blind Spot of Fear.

Anyone can feel abandoned if you live by family, the same friends for many years, and then all of a sudden you have to move to another town, or even another state because either you or your spouse has a transfer in the work field.

Some people tend to believe that since the family is now far away, and the old friends are no longer available to fellowship with, confide in, that the new set of friends will someday also abandon them. They might even tend to feel the same way towards God.

What does the God of the Bible say?

"Do not Fear" appears over 100 times in God's word. Some would even say there is one for each day of the year, and the most often reason given is the Lord's words, "For I am with you!" Or some phrase similar in meaning.

> *So do not fear, for I am with you; do not be dismayed, for I am your God. I will strengthen you and help you; I will uphold you with my righteous right hand* (Isaiah 41:10).

> *For all who are led by the Spirit of God are children of God. 15 For you did not receive a spirit of slavery to fall back into fear, but you have received a spirit of adoption. When we cry, "Abba! Father!" 16 it is that very Spirit bearing witness with our spirit that we are children of God, 17 and if children, then heirs, heirs of God and joint heirs with Christ—if, in fact, we suffer with him so that we may also be glorified with him* (Romans 8:14-17a, NRSV).

> *But in all these things we overwhelmingly conquer through Him who loved us. 38 For I am convinced that neither death, nor life, nor angels, nor principalities, nor things present, nor things to come, nor powers, 39 nor height, nor depth, nor any other created thing, will be able to separate us from the love of God, which is in Christ Jesus our Lord* (Romans 8:37-39, NASB).

Caution is a God-given mechanism we are born with to warn us of danger. With that said:

> *The fear of the Lord is the beginning of wisdom, and knowledge of the Holy One understands* (Proverbs 9:10).

> *Whoever fears the LORD has a secure fortress, and for their children it will be a refuge* (Proverbs 14:26).

As followers of Jesus, we need to have a healthy and respectful fear in our life.

> *The fear of the LORD is the beginning of wisdom; prudent are all who live by it. Your praise endures forever* (Psalm 111:10).

As you read these next two life stories, you will see how a Blind Spot of Fear could have entered my life at an early age.

At age nine, convinced that I could parachute, I threw my bedsheet over my shoulder and climbed the tree next to our house, to my brother's and my treehouse. Once I'd made the ascent, I looked down at the roof of our house. It appeared to be a safer place from which to jump. So, I jumped from the treehouse to the house.

If my parents had been home and had known where I was, they would have grounded me for life. As I stood there on our roof, I remember feeling that I not only shouldn't have been on the roof, nor should I have even contemplated jumping from the roof. The fear of jumping provoked a quick but fleeting thought, "don't jump––you could get hurt."

After what seemed like forever, I finally walked to the edge of the roof and stared down at the ground, believing that my bed sheet would form a perfect parachute and significantly soften my landing. After all, I had watched many army movies on TV and at the theater. I'd seen men parachute from airplanes. They always landed just fine.

Even though I was fearful, I grabbed the four corners of my bed sheet, and jumped. As gravity would have it, I hit the ground on both feet hard enough to jar my entire body like a mountain experiencing an 8.5 magnitude earthquake. My knees buckled into a full crouching position.

Looking back now, I realize that it was by the grace of God, which I understand now, as an adult that the only thing hurt was my selfish pride. After gathering my thoughts and standing straight up, I came to my senses and realized I wasn't physically hurt. As I shook like a leaf in a tree during a windstorm, I put one foot in front of the other, as I made my way to the back door of our home. The only fear left now for me was if my parents had known. I immediately snuck in through the back door with my bed sheet all bunched up, holding it behind my back with one hand, as I avoided being seen by my brother Barry, who was also home at the time.

Three years previous, I was only six years old and living in Kitzingen, Germany with my parents and two siblings on an American army base where I was born.

One day while out on the apartment playground, I began to watch as some city workers across the street were laying red clay pipe in a ditch they had prepared with a giant backhoe. As the men working drove away from the work site, I then walked over and looked down into the ditch that didn't appear very wide to jump across.

As a hyper and curious youngster, I began jumping across the ditch as I turned around and repeatedly jumped back and forth several times. I remember how freeing and courageous it felt to make it across the ditch more than once.

The very next thing I experienced was waking up and looking up at a man's face I had never seen before. A scary fear came over me as I soon realized this man with the unfamiliar face was carrying me draped across his arms as he asked me where I lived.

For some reason, I felt perplexed and disoriented, and I wasn't able to explain what apartment I lived in with my family. This man, while carrying me in his arms, began a journey knocking on doors to see whom I belonged to in the apartment complex. Other than the knocking noise on each apartment door and the noise of his shoes on the sidewalk, it was hushed, as if time had stood still.

The very next noise I hear is my mom's voice. As I look up and see her face, all the fear I felt when this man carried me had somehow left.

Later that day, after a trip to the local army hospital for what seemed like a tapestry of stitches in the back of my head, my mom explained things to me. A sanitation worker found me in the ditch, then carried me from apartment to apartment until he found ours. On his daily route, as he drove by, he looked out of his garbage truck window and saw me laying "lifelessly" in the ditch.

While I had been jumping back and forth across the ditch, I must have slipped and fallen backward because the back of my head hit the red clay pipe, splitting wide open like a watermelon thrown onto concrete from a tall building.

If a Blind Spot of Fear had entered in my life back then, I wouldn't have been in construction climbing on roofs, digging ditches, as I did later in adulthood in the construction field.

> As Frederick W. Cropp, once said, "There is much in the world to make us afraid. There is more in our faith to make us unafraid."

Many years later, it was just a typical day as my mother sat in her car at a stop sign waiting for her turn to proceed to her destination. This stop sign was the same stop sign my mom had occupied many times over the years as it is on the only road to the store in which she traveled that day.

Suddenly, a man on a motorcycle sped through the intersection and couldn't make his attempted left turn. In this man's ridiculous driving, not only did he miss his left turn but also the motorcycle went out of control. He remained on it for a short time but later fell over sliding beneath my mom's car.

As if my mom wasn't already scared and upset enough from what had just occurred, she became even more devastated when the man riding the motorcycle stood up and started screaming at her as if it was her fault. Though it was a minor accident and my mom and the person on the bike were unharmed, other than emotionally, it caused my mom a deep-gripping fear.

Even though my mom didn't recognize it, she ended up with a bad case of fear. It was more than just False Evidence Appearing Real; it was a fear that was gripping and devastating and became a Blind Spot of Fear that took away the freedom of my mom feeling safe to drive again.

Some people I have personally known—and perhaps people you have known or still know, have struggled with fear for years. If this describes your season of life that you are currently experiencing, then hopefully through time you can eventually begin to find that the things that once sent you down a fearful spiral will no longer have the same effect. It may not happen quickly, but over days, months, and even years, it can certainly change, if you're willing to put the hard work in searching out the reason why you are in or have been in a season of fear.

One of my dear friends was driving on a very windy dangerous road in Ramona California, where throughout the year and for many years has been a road that experiences minor, major, and fatal accidents. As my friend was driving home, an oncoming car came across into her lane and hit her as it caused her SUV to flip in mid-air several times. Fortunately, by God's grace, her vehicle landed on all four wheels.

Almost immediately following the accident, which totaled her SUV, she had allowed a Blind Spot of Fear to birth without realizing it. The Blind Spot of Fear led to anxiousness, and she was unable to travel the windy road for a period to go to town. When she began driving again, she chose a different and longer route to drive to town to purchase groceries or go to work. Days, weeks, and months went by as she began to embrace Scriptures on fear, deep healing prayer times, along with some in-depth discussions about the Blind Spot of Fear itself. In time she was able to resolve her Blind Spot of Fear and conquered the same windy road again. (See Anxiety & Worry in Chapter 5.)

> *So you can be assured, God is with you in whatever you face, in the turmoil and struggles of fear in life. God is there, strengthening, helping, and He holds you in His hands* (1 Peter 3:14).

Here are some suggestive steps you can to take to combat the Blind Spot of Fear:

1. Do not allow fear to control your life.

Feelings are not right or wrong; they are what they are! Even though you might still feel afraid, you can believe and have faith that God is with you. You may not be in control, but you can trust the One who is. You can't know the future, but you can know the God who does.

As you continue to read, you will see Scriptures to back all this up.

2. Guard your heart.

Read God's words of life and truth over and over, praying them out loud until they replace the other things in your mind that plague you. There's nothing magical about God's word, but instead, His words are majestic. The verses have power through them because they are His words.

Even though fear is sometimes still present, as change begins to happen, that fear should no longer have a steady grip holding you back and paralyzing you in its grasp.

God's words can take root to reveal and bring new life that's soothing to the soul and calming to our spirits as it gives power to our hours, our days, our months and years to come. It's not always easy, and it often comes down to one or more choices:

3. Focus on what the true is in uncertain times.

God is great, and His power helps us to live courageous, boldly and fearlessly in this life while many things that surround us would tell us to be afraid.

Please, pause for a few minutes and circle at least one or more of these Scripture references below. Look them up to read and ponder them for a few minutes and at the end of this chapter, or after you finish reading my book, go back and look them up on your cell phone, iPad or laptop to read and ponder the ones you didn't circle.

Old Testament: *Deuteronomy* 3:22, *Joshua* 1:9, *Psalm* 23:4, 27:1, 34:4, 34:7, 46:1.

New Testament: *Mark* 5:36, John 14:27, *Romans* 8:38.

Questions to ponder and room to write as you leave this chapter!

How was this chapter helpful in my current circumstances?

_____
_____
_____

What Fear do I have right now?

_____
_____
_____

Including God, what relationships have I pushed away due to my Fear?

_____
_____
_____

What are my next steps to move towards freedom from my Fear?

_____
_____
_____

Before entering the next chapter Anxiety & Worry, please pause and pray this prayer:

Father God, thank you for highlighting and revealing my Blind Spot of Fear.

Father God, I now realize that Fear can hold me back from experiencing all you have planned for me. I want to live in all your promises and plans for my life!

> *For I know the plans I have for you," declares the Lord, "plans to prosper you and not to harm you, plans to give you hope and a future* (Jeremiah 29:11)

Father God teach me not to fear, and as I release all of the stuff on my mind right now, I give it all to You.

Thank you, Holy Spirit, for replacing those fearful thoughts with your words of Your truth. You know what concerns me! I ask You to help me focus my mind on what truth is no matter what my circumstances are.

Father God, I realize just reading this book is not enough for total healing, so I pray that you will place the right pastors, leaders, counselors, and friends who understand me in my life to walk the rest of this healing journey with me.

Help me to sleep fearlessly tonight.

I pray these things in Jesus name! Amen.

> "The person of the Holy Spirit speaks quiet truths that are as pure as the nectar a bee extracts from a beautiful single rose on a lonely hillside." -- **Pastor Mark Baxter**

As you continue to read this book, I pray as you seek God that he will not only heal your past Fear, but he will help you in your present walk and journey with Him as you head into the future.

Remember, God is always pursuing a deeper and more intimate relationship with you.

Your new friend,

Pastor Mark

Chapter 5
Anxiety & Worry

"Worry is calling God's integrity into question."
--Eddie Smith

This chapter will cover just some of the ways of navigating through daily, weekly or even years of past, and present Anxiety & Worry. When you know who you are in Christ, anxiety, and worry can be easy to navigate with some counsel, prayer and or reading some scriptures that deal with the issue.

However, if you aren't able to navigate so quickly through your anxiety and worry, you may have a Blind Spot of Anxiety & Worry that may or may not be rooted in a Blind Spot of Fear in Chapter 4.

In Chapter 2, I explained how one of Satan's most popular and powerful weapons that he uses against us is Fear! This chapter will focus on two emotions that can overwhelm us and similarly, like fear, can cause a thick shadow of darkness that sometimes controls our daily lives and routines.

By the way, if you are wondering? Yes, Satan also plays on the playground of Anxiety & Worry.

What is anxiety & worry?

Anxiety:

Anxiety is a feeling of nervousness that is typically about an imminent event or something with an uncertain outcome.

Worry:

Worry is an unease allowing one's mind to dwell on difficulty or trouble in a circumstance.

You probably have heard the saying, "Let's not make a mountain out of a molehill." If you're not familiar with molehills, they are little mounds of dirt derived from a varmint that burrows in the ground like a gopher. A molehill is small and can quickly be flattened and destroyed with just one hand or foot.

When you have a Blind Spot of Anxiety & Worry, Satan can plague your mind with past Anxiety & Worry bringing those thoughts into your present situation to cause your actions to exaggerate everything, small, medium or large, to the point where it seems like the world is caving in on you.

When this action is happening, the doors are open for Satan to plague you by the "What if's?"

- What if I get laid off from work?
- What if my house gets burglarized?
- What if I lose my home in an earthquake, a fire, a tornado or a hurricane?
- What if my health fails?
- What if one of my family members dies?
- What if's can go on and on and on!

Let's face it, from the time you climb out of bed, and until you return to that same bed, your life can become all about Worry.

However, reality sets in when we realize that almost 90 percent of what we spend our time worrying about never materializes!

I came up with this quote in 1995 when a close friend of mine was in constant worry about something.

"Worry not! Pray a lot!" -- **Pastor Mark Baxter**

"Worry is a thin stream of fear trickling through the mind. If encouraged, it cuts a channel into which all other thoughts are drained."

– **Arthur Somers Roche**

"My life has been full of terrible misfortunes -- most of which have never happened."

– **Michel de Montaigne**

A favorite saying both my parents quoted growing up: "Let's cross that bridge when it happens!"

One unique key is choosing to focus your mind on the truth, even when storms of life and frustrating circumstances arise that you can't figure out or immediately resolve.

What is the truth?

Truth is God's Word, both read and revealed:

For instance, look at Peter's story. When he encountered Jesus walking on the water, he was afraid.

> *Immediately he made the disciples get into the boat and go on ahead to the other side, while he dismissed the crowds. 23 And after he had dismissed the crowds, he went up the mountain by himself to pray. When evening came, he was there alone, 24 but by this time the boat, battered by the waves, was far from the land, for the wind was against them. 25 And early in the morning he came walking towards them on the lake. 26 But when the disciples saw him walking on the lake, they were terrified, saying, 'It is a ghost!' And they cried out in fear. 27 But immediately Jesus spoke to them and said, 'Take*

> *heart, it is I; do not be afraid.'* 28 *Peter answered him, 'Lord, if it is you, command me to come to you on the water.'* 29 *He said, 'Come.' So Peter got out of the boat, started walking on the water, and came towards Jesus.* 30 *But when he noticed the strong wind, he became frightened, and beginning to sink, he cried out, 'Lord, save me!'* 31 *Jesus immediately reached out his hand and caught him, saying to him, 'You of little faith, why did you doubt?'* 32 *When they got into the boat, the wind ceased.* 33 *And those in the boat worshipped him, saying, 'Truly you are the Son of God'* (Matthew 14:22-33).

Notice in that narrative how Peter got anxious to leave the boat as he was so worried about it sinking. He felt that if Jesus commanded him to come, he would be safe! He felt safe until his focus changed from his eyes being on Jesus to the waves overtaking him. Let's remember to keep our eyes on Jesus! When our eyes are focused on Jesus, our circumstance gets smaller, and Jesus gets more prominent than the problem that is trying to overtake us.

> *I have told you these things, so that in me you may have peace. In this world you will have trouble. But take heart! I have overcome the world* (John 16:33).

There are lots of things to be anxious about, like abductions, crime, economic uncertainty, terrorism, violence, and wars.

When we set our focus on one or several of the above, it gives an opportunity for Anxiety to establish itself, that can lead to Worry that begins to plague us.

When we think of our children's future along with our future, we can become financially anxious, which leads to worry that can grow in our present heading towards our future.

Cast all your anxiety on him because he cares for you (1 Peter 5:7).

A child once made these comments: My mother is such a worrier—one cough and she thinks I've got bronchitis. One headache and she thinks I've got a brain tumor.

My wife and I lost our home to the " 2007 Witch Creek Fire" in Ramona California. The fires of 2007 were some of the most devastating fires in California history.

As we waited in line at the emergency relief center to receive supplies to sustain us, we both encountered a lady that had also lost her home in the same fire. I'm sharing this particular story because she was a woman that lived in fear that led her to Anxiety & Worry. (See Fear in Chapter 4.)

I want you to see something else here; this woman had just lost her home in the 2007 fire, but sadly in August 2005 she had also lost her previous home in the Katrina Hurricane. After the loss of her home in New Orleans, she had allowed two Blind Spots to enter her life, which were a Blind Spot of Fear and a Blind Spot of Anxiety & Worry. She figured if she moved out of New Orleans she would be safe. She moved to beautiful San Diego, California, out to the little country town of Ramona. She was entirely out of hurricane alley so that she would be out of harm's way and her house would be safe unless a major earthquake hit San Diego.

However, this was not the case for her as she had then lost her second home to another natural tragedy, i.e., the 2007 "Witch Creek Fire," as she found that moving out of hurricane alley was not foolproof enough.

My wife and I had the incredible privilege to come alongside her at that very moment as we prayed for her, but as we dealt with our loss and what happens along with that process, we never saw the woman again after that day.

The absolute saddest part to this woman's story is she used her insurance money from Katrina and paid cash for her home in Ramona but did not purchase insurance for it. She told us that she dreaded the long process ahead of dealing with FEMA.

Especially when tragedy hits, we all need to remember to speak life to others and ourselves, too.

> *The tongue has the power of life and death, and those who love it will eat its fruit* (Proverbs 18:21).

God's word on worry:

> *Therefore I tell you, do not worry about your life, what you will eat or drink; or about your body, what you will wear. Is not life more than food, and the body more than clothes? 26 Look at the birds of the air; they do not sow or reap or store away in barns, and yet your heavenly Father feeds them. Are you not much more valuable than they? 27 Can any one of you by worrying add a single hour to your life?* (Matthew 6:25-27).

For more on worry, you can continue to read the rest of this chapter through *Matthew* 6:28-34.

God's word on anxious thoughts:

> *Be anxious for nothing, but in everything by prayer and supplication with thanksgiving let your requests be made known to God* (Philippians 4:6, NASB).

After all, we have a Big God who heals. One way to receive His healing is to read His Word, over and over, praying the verses aloud until they become so familiar to us that they replace the other things we have believed. God's Word is majestic and brings lasting results.

> When we embrace this passage of Scripture and begin to apply it to our lives, change happens! *Do not conform to the pattern of this world, but be transformed by the renewing of your mind. Then you will be able to test and approve what God's will is— his good, pleasing and perfect will* (Romans 12:2).

Anxious thoughts diminish as they let go of the constant grip they once had. Even though thoughts of Anxiety can still arise, they no longer take control of you, cause worry, and hold you back from your normal daily routines, or the fun you used to miss out on because of it.

God's words are words of life that comfort our soul, bringing calm to our inner man/woman and give us power for our days ahead. It's not always easy, and it often comes down to believing what God says instead of what we observe or think we see!

We might still have anxious thoughts and worry too, but we can trust the One who is Large and in Charge and entirely in control. We may not know the future. But we can know the God who does. God is with you in whatever you face, in the turmoil, struggles within anxious thoughts and the worries of life.

Jesus appeared to sweat drops of blood in the garden of Gethsemane from the anxiety that arose from thoughts of hanging on the cross.

> *And being in anguish, he prayed more earnestly, and his sweat was like drops of blood falling to the ground* (Luke 22:4).

However, Jesus chose to follow the Father's will and not his own so you can be entirely sure that Jesus is at the right hand of the Father, interceding and strengthening you by helping you hold your hands and arms up when they get weary from Anxiety that can lead to Worry!

God's Word gives us the power of a sound mind & boldness without anxiety & worry in this life, even when many circumstances surround us would tell us the exact opposite. God's truth speaks to every living cell in us and into the deepest core of our spirits.

Please pause circle or highlight one or more of these scriptures, and look up, read, and ponder at least one: *Psalm* 46:1, *Psalm* 55:22, *Psalm* 94:19, *Philippians* 4:6-7, or 1 *Peter* 5:7.

Whether you are fishing with a line or casting a net, both are a form of casting. Picture yourself throwing your Anxiety away and catching the peace of God in exchange. Once we have the peace of God, we can then become fishers of men.

> *"Come, follow me," Jesus said, "and I will send you out to fish for people* (Mathew 4:19).

Questions to ponder as you leave this chapter!

How was this chapter helpful in my current circumstances?

_____
_____
_____
_____

What is the Anxiety I'm experiencing right now?

_____
_____
_____
_____

What is the Worry I feel right now?

_____
_____
_____
_____

What are my next steps to move towards freedom from Anxiety?

_____
_____
_____
_____

What are my next steps to move towards freedom from Worry?

_____
_____
_____
_____

God already knows your Anxiety level and wants to hear you talk to Him about it.

Before entering the next chapter on Offense, please pray this prayer:

Father God, thank you for highlighting and revealing my Blind Spot of Anxiety & Worry

I choose to listen to Your Word on Anxiety.

> *Do not be anxious about anything, but in every situation, by prayer and petition, with thanksgiving, present your requests to God* (Philippians 4:6).

Father, I thank you for what You say about Worry, and I refuse to let it control my life anymore.

> *Consider the ravens: They do not sow or reap, they have no storeroom or barn; yet God feeds them. And how much more valuable you are than birds!* (Luke 12:24).

As I continue to walk out my journey in healing with you, Holy Spirit, please prompt me to read your Word as you open the door for me to take steps to dissolve the damage done to my relationships.

Father God, I realize just reading this book is not enough for total healing, so I pray that you will place the right pastors, leaders, counselors, and friends who understand me to walk the rest of this healing journey with me.

Help me with any anxious or worrisome thoughts as I lay my head on my pillow tonight.

I pray these things in Jesus name! Amen.

I pray that as you pray and seek God in this journey of healing, that he will not only heal your past hurts and damaged relationships, but he will also help you in your present, heading into the future. Remember, God is always pursuing a deeper and more intimate relationship with you.

Your new friend,

Pastor Mark

Chapter 6
Offense

"Trials in this life will expose what is in your heart—whether the offense is toward God or others. Tests either make you bitter toward God and your peers or stronger. If you pass the test, your roots will shoot down deeper, stabilizing you and your future. If you fail, you become offended, which can lead to defilement with bitterness."

— **John Bevere,** *The Bait of Satan: Living Free from the Deadly Trap of Offense*

What is an offense?

An offense is an annoyance or resentment brought about by a perceived insult to or disregard for oneself or one's standards or principles.

Before we get deeper into this chapter, let me ask this question?

Why do the fish in rivers, lakes, and oceans keep getting bigger, Bigger, & even BIGGER?

The answer that I want us to get here is: *Because the fish see the hook and not the bait*!

So, what is it that I am trying to say?

> Satan, "dangles daily carrots, but we aren't rabbits and horses, and we don't have to bite them, eat them and swallow them." -- **Pastor Mark Baxter**

The subject of offense has been hindering many Christian as well as non-followers of Jesus in people's life journeys for centuries!

As believers and followers of Jesus we need to embrace these following scriptures:

> *If it is possible, as far as it depends on you, live at peace with everyone* (Romans 12:18).
>
> *If any of you lacks wisdom, you should ask God, who gives generously to all without finding fault, and it will be given to you* (James 1:5).

Let's face this fact of life! We have all been guilty of offending others either knowingly or unknowingly.

We can all offend followers of Jesus as well as non-followers of Jesus and even God too!

- Pause here for a minute and consider this question. How many people do you think you offended unintentionally growing up in school?

- What about the times you left people out because you didn't think they fit into your category of friends?

- What about times when sports teams got picked, and you only chose the ones that could run fast or could throw or catch well?

- What about a school dance as you walked up to ask someone to dance, and you walked right past someone that was expecting you to ask them to dance?

As a pastor in my journey of life, I recognize as I write this book that I probably have non-intentionally offended more people than I can imagine.

While pastoring my church in Ramona, California from 2012 – 2016, I had an older married couple as parishioners that would stay home from church if I, the senior pastor, didn't say hi, or shake their hand on the previous Sunday morning. After finding this out and even though this married couple had been Christians for well over 30, years I began to understand that it was their insecurities that caused them to bite the bait of an offense that was 100 percent non-intentional by me as their pastor.

When people are part of a tight-knit family/community at church for a long time, they should be connected enough not to feel like they had to be singled out and talked to by the pastor every time the church doors are open.

This married couple somehow had bit the bait and allowed a Blind Spot of Offense to enter their lives many years beforehand, which later birthed a Transference Blind Spot (See Blind Spot Transference in Chapter 7).

I found out later that when this couple heard a pastor say something from the pulpit with which they disagreed, they would leave the church, and go to another one. They continued this pattern, church after church! These people were so busy looking for the perfect church that they never resolved their Blind Spot of Offense. There is no perfect church, only a perfect Jesus. Had they found a perfect church and joined it, it would no longer be perfect.

The Blind Spot of Offense can go much more-in-depth at times. Let me explain; there are times when a person(s) will pick up or take someone else's offense. It happens when the person thinks they are protecting or fighting the battle for the person that the perceived adverse action(s) is intended. Sometimes the reason this happens, there is a Blind Spot of Transference in that person's life, as you will read in the next chapter.

> *Good sense makes one slow to anger, and it is his glory to overlook an offense* (Proverbs 19:11, ESV).

In this Bible narrative, King David is repenting for offending God.

> 1 *Have mercy on me, O God,*
> *according to your unfailing love;*
> *according to your great compassion*
> *blot out my transgressions.*
> 2 *Wash away all my iniquity*
> *and cleanse me from my sin.*
> 3 *For I know my transgressions,*
> *and my sin is always before me.*
> 4 *Against you, you only, have I sinned*
> *and done what is evil in your sight;*
> *so you are right in your verdict*
> *and justified when you judge.*
> 5 *Surely I was sinful at birth,*
> *sinful from the time my mother conceived me.*
> 6 *Yet you desired faithfulness even in the womb;*
> *you taught me wisdom in that secret place.*
> 7 *Cleanse me with hyssop, and I will be clean;*
> *wash me, and I will be whiter than snow.*

8 *Let me hear joy and gladness;*
let the bones you have crushed rejoice.
9 *Hide your face from my sins*
and blot out all my iniquity.
10 *Create in me a pure heart, O God,*
and renew a steadfast spirit within me.
11 *Do not cast me from your presence*
or take your Holy Spirit from me.
12 *Restore to me the joy of your salvation*
and grant me a willing spirit, to sustain me.
13 *Then I will teach transgressors your ways,*
so that sinners will turn back to you.
14 *Deliver me from the guilt of bloodshed, O God,*
you who are God my Savior,
and my tongue will sing of your righteousness.
15 *Open my lips, Lord,*
and my mouth will declare your praise.
16 *You do not delight in sacrifice,*
or I would bring it;
you do not take pleasure in burnt offerings.
17 *My sacrifice, O God, is a broken spirit;*
a broken and contrite heart
you, God, will not despise.
18 *May it please you to prosper Zion,*

> *to build up the walls of Jerusalem.*
> *19 Then you will delight in the sacrifices of*
> *the righteous,*
> *in burnt offerings offered whole;*
> *then bulls will be offered on your altar*
> (Psalm 51:1-19.

I asked you to read that Scripture, because believers and non-believers can offend us, and we as believers and followers of Christ can offend God if we have one of these "Blind Spots; see Arrogance in Chapter 10, Pride & Rebellion in Chapter 9 or Unforgiveness in Chapter 17.

There will be times in life where we will all experience being offended, and when it does happen, wouldn't be great if we could quickly grow rhino skin or be like a duck as water repels off its back.

God's words give life and soothe our souls as they also calm our spirits and provide power to our daily lives. A change will happen when we read, believe and apply God's word.

> *Do not pay attention to every word people say, or you may hear your servant cursing you—22 for you know in your heart that many times you yourself have cursed others* (Ecclesiastes 7:21-22).

> *So if you are offering your gift at the altar and there remember that your brother has something against you, 24 leave your gift there before the altar and go. First be reconciled to your brother, and then come and offer your gift. 25 Come to terms quickly with your accuser while you are going with him to court, lest your accuser hand you over to the judge, and the*

judge to the guard, and you be put in prison (Matthew 5:23-25, ESV).

In the future remember to look for the Hook and don't bite the Bait!

Questions to ponder as you leave this chapter!

How was this chapter helpful in my current circumstances?

_____
_____
_____
_____

What Offense(s) do I need to resolve?

_____
_____
_____
_____

Who have I Offended?

_____
_____
_____
_____

What Offense(s) have I taken on that weren't mine?

_____
_____

What are my next steps to move towards freedom from carrying an Offense(s)?

Remember

God invites us to come to Him 24/7 with any of our life issues. He knows our pain and wants to hear our voices, so He can heal us emotionally, physically, and spiritually!

Before entering the next chapter on Transference, please pause and pray this prayer:

Father God, thank you for highlighting and revealing my Blind Spot of Offense.

> "If we don't risk being hurt, we cannot give unconditional love. Unconditional love gives others the right to hurt us."
>
> **— John Bevere, Bait Of Satan: Living Free from the Deadly Trap of Offense**

Thank you, Holy Spirit, for replacing those thoughts of Offense with the scriptures in the Bible concerning this matter.

> *A person's wisdom yields patience;*
> *it is to one's glory to overlook an offense*
> (Proverbs 19:11).

Father God, I realize just reading this book is not enough for total healing, so I pray that you will place the right pastors, leaders, counselors, and friends who understand me to walk the rest of this healing journey with me.

I pray these things in Jesus name! Amen.

I pray as you seek God in this, that he will not only heal your past, but he will help you in your present heading into the future. Remember, God is always pursuing and deepening his relationship with you.

Your new friend,

Pastor Mark

Part 3

Blind Spots That Can Manipulate Relationships

Chapter 7
Transference

When the word *transference* is used, we think it only has to do with people.

After my friend Bill's dog past from old age, he went to a local animal rescue and picked up an 8-month-old Labrador retriever and named him Spot; as he had only one white spot on his tail.

Bill wanted to train his new puppy as he had his last dog. He started out teaching Spot how to shake, sit, and lay down with one command for each. He taught him how to fetch sticks and tennis balls. He also taught Spot how to fetch his slippers, but when he tried to teach him to fetch the morning newspaper, Spot ran, and hid on the opposite side of the house. Bill thinking Spot was just playing, walked over to him with the newspaper, and Spot ran this time, into the house through the front doggie door. Bill figured it out; Spot's previous owner must have disciplined him with the newspaper. Spot had picked up a Transference Blind Spot and thought Bill was going to hit him with the newspaper too.

What is transference?

Transference is the redirection of feelings and desires and especially of those unconsciously retained from childhood toward a new object.

As you continue your journey in this book, you will see Satan has lots of stuff to throw at us to remind us of past and present hurts. We all get hurt, and when we do, we need Scripture passages to give us insight. God says, *If any of you lacks wisdom, you should ask God, who gives generously to all without finding fault, and it will be given to you* (James 1:5).

One Greek word we would see for this is, the word *Metaphora,* which translates to words like transfer, which derives from transference or the English word transport, which comes from the phrase transportation or to carry!

Two emotional components can play into and fuel Transference.

- The first one is projection, which is an estimate or forecast of a future situation or trend based on a study of present ones.

- The second one is repression, which is the action of subduing someone or something by force.

There are times where repressed feelings will be pushed back so deep that they finally explode onto our loved ones!

As a pastor, it is an absolute proven fact that negative Transference is 100% inescapable in ministry.

Here are just two examples:

- Many sermons have explained tithes and offerings. Messages are preached all the time about the privilege of sowing into God's kingdom. When some families tithe 10 percent of their wages for the first time, the next week their car breaks down, or their washer and dryer quit working. They immediately go into the transference mode, projecting their anger towards their pastors and God. They do this because the pastors have shared how the Bible is true and that God always provides for his people.

- There were many times I would preach a sermon that really opened the eyes of someone's heart wounds and now all of a sudden that person might begin to view me as an, e.g., stepfather or uncle that they once hated. A Blind Spot of Transference from the past of old repressed thoughts of their father, mother, stepfather, stepmother, uncle or aunt or even a previous schoolteacher project on to me in the pulpit.

In the previous chapter on the Blind Spot Offense, I shared a story about a longtime older church-going couple and how earlier in their life they had bit the bait of offense. Because of them not seeing the hook that snagged both, a Blind Spot of Transference is formed in their lives.

In 1 Samuel 30:6, we find a perfect example of Transference,

David was greatly distressed because the men were talking of stoning him; each one was bitter in spirit because of his sons and daughters. But David found strength in the Lord his God.

The very men that David commanded and fought with battle after battle and now had wept with—because all of them had lost everything to the Amalekites in Verses 1-5 of 1 Samuel chapter 30; now wanted to stone him to death. David's fighting men had turned to Transference as their repressed raw emotions against the Amalekites were being projected as anger onto David.

We are created to walk in Shalom (the peace of God).

The word Shalom is the Hebrew word that can be used idiomatically to mean both hello and goodbye. However, the much more profound meaning is peace and harmony, wholeness, completeness, prosperity, welfare, and tranquility.

What feelings have you repressed that you tend to use in negative Transference towards others? There is a place at the end of this chapter to write those out.

There is also positive transference,

Jesus transferred all that we deserved to Himself, as he was scourged, and our sin was placed on Him at the cross.

Jesus transferred all His authority; His Rule & Reign onto us by and through the Holy Spirit, so that we could walk in His power and authority to witness and cast out demons and heal the sick.

Questions to ponder and room to write as you leave this chapter!

How was this chapter helpful in my current circumstances?

_____
_____
_____
_____

How am I a recipient of Transference?

_____
_____
_____
_____

How am I stuck in Transference mode?

_____
_____
_____
_____

What are my next steps to move towards freedom from Transference?

_____
_____
_____
_____

Before entering the next chapter on Foolishness, please pause and pray this prayer:

Father God, thank you for highlighting and revealing my Blind Spot of Transference and how damaging transference can be.

Thank you for all of your words of truth. You know what concerns me; I choose to guard my heart, not to allow Transference to control my life, and to now focus my mind on what truth is in the midst of storms I may face.

Lord Jesus, I realize just reading this book is not enough for total healing, so I pray that you will place the right pastors, leaders, counselors, and friends who understand me to walk the rest of this healing journey with me.

I pray these things in Jesus name! Amen.

I pray as you seek God in this, that he will not only heal your past, but he will help you in your present heading into the future. Remember, God is always pursuing and deepening his relationship with you.

Your new friend,

Pastor Mark

Chapter 8
Foolishness

In my senior year of high school, one Friday night, all my friends were cruising. I didn't yet have my driver's license, as I had broken my leg in two places below the knee, at the beginning of summer.

My friend Tim had turned sixteen and bought himself a '67 Chevrolet Impala with money he earned over the summer while I was laid up with my broken leg.

I asked my dad if I could go cruising with my friends, Donald, Tim, and Steve, and my dad said no. He knew all three of them well. I kept asking to go, over, and over again. My got tired of me asking, and finally said yes, but if you get arrested; and he said no more! My dad had wisdom and was right most of the time, and once again he was right, as Donald's, Tim's, Steve's foolishness, and mine got us arrested.

What is foolishness?

A foolish person is one who acts unwisely or imprudently, which can be a silly person.

Please pause here and look up these short scriptures:

- The silly fool (Proverbs 1:7)
- The scorning fool (Proverbs 13:1)

But God chose the foolish things of the world to shame the wise; God chose the weak things of the world to shame the strong (1 Corinthians 1:27).

Over twenty years ago and after meeting friends that attended Vineyard churches, I found that I loved the way they worshiped God as they sang to Him and not just songs about Him. I also witnessed the way they loved the unloved in their communities.

In just a short time attending a Vineyard church, I began to hear some coined phrases by the Vineyard church founder and planter John Wimber. One of my favorites was:

"I'm a fool for Christ—whose fool are you?"

– John Wimber

We are fools for Christ, but you are so wise in Christ! We are weak, but you are strong! You are honored, we are dishonored (1 Corinthians 4:10).

So, as a follower of Jesus, if we are going to be foolish, let's do it positively to further the kingdom of God as He uses us to continue to confound the wise.

I gave my life to Christ when I was 16-years-old at the San Diego Jack Murphy Stadium. After I graduated high school, I moved to northern California with a pastor's family. I went to church every Wednesday night, Sunday morning, and Sunday evening.

I sang in a men's quartet with two of the pastor's sons and another friend from high school that moved with us to northern California. We called the group, "Christian Brothers," as we visited a local men's prison in a nearby town. We each shared our testimonies and how Christ had changed our lives. I remember one night while singing at the prison, a man gave his life to Christ, and once released from prison, he brought his wife and kids to our church with him.

Even though I lived with a pastor's family, I wasn't told to read the Bible and pray every day, nor did anyone at the church ever ask to disciple or mentor me either.

Just shy of my 22nd birthday, I moved back to San Diego County and hooked up with several of the guys I graduated high school with in 1975. Along with Donald, Tim, and Steve, there were others too.

Due to the fact of not being near my church community and my friends being party animals, I soon walked away from God and the church. After being deceived by my desires, a Blind Spot of Foolishness set in as I began a 17 and one-half year foolish journey of partying hard with drugs, alcohol, and everything that goes with that lifestyle.

My foolish behavior led me to spend a great deal of money in the bars and buying party essentials to attract people on the same path I was on. I remember all my high school friends that were not in my party circle had all gotten married. Some of them had already purchased homes, and some owned very successful businesses. Even though I saw, heard, and witnessed how good they were all doing, I continued walking in my Foolishness Blind Spot for many years.

The fool says in his heart, "There is no God." They are corrupt, doing abominable iniquity; there is none who does good (Psalm 14:1, ESV).

Even though I didn't verbalize it, my actions stated the previous verse!

Questions to ponder and room to write as you leave this chapter!

How was this chapter helpful in my current circumstances?

_____
_____
_____
_____

How is my speech towards others Foolishness?

_____
_____
_____
_____

What decisions have I made lately that led to Foolishness?

_____
_____
_____
_____

What are my next steps to move towards freedom from Foolishness?

_____
_____
_____
_____

Before entering the next chapter on Pride & Rebellion, please pause and pray this prayer:

Father God, thank you for highlighting and revealing my Blind Spot of Foolishness

> *While we look not at the things which are seen, but at the things which are not seen: for the things which are seen are temporal; but the things which are not seen are eternal* (2 Corinthians 4:18, KJV).

Lord, thank you that now I can see how Foolishness can lead to a destructive lifestyle, such as spending money on foolish things that are only temporary, and following idols leading to darkness.

Thank you, Holy Spirit, for replacing thoughts of Foolishness with your words of truth. You know what concerns me; I know you go before me and you have my back.

I realize just reading this book is not enough for total healing, so I pray that you will place the right pastors, leaders, counselors, and friends who understand me to walk the rest of this healing journey with me.

I pray these things in Jesus name! Amen.

I pray as you seek God in this, that he will not only heal your past, but he will help you in your present heading into the future. Remember, God is always pursuing and deepening his relationship with you.

Your new friend,

Pastor Mark

Chapter 9
Pride & Rebellion

Frank was an avid rock climber, and a very good one at that, and had ascended many high mountains with rather dangerous sheer cliffs. However, Frank also thought he was the best climber around. He along with a group of his friends set out for a weekend climb. When they arrived, they surveyed the prospective areas to climb. They all had fun, and each one of them conquered each challenging peak except one! Frank, in his pride, tried to convince everyone to climb the one peak that they unanimously felt was too extensive for their climbing abilities, but each one declined the invitation, and they all headed back home.

The next day Frank called in sick at work and headed back out to climb that peak. Frank had made two mistakes that day, he was in rebellion as he lied to his boss about being sick, he went climbing alone with no spotter, and he was attempting something that was very dangerous alone. He made it part way up the peak, hit a spot that was to difficult to climb, but in his pride decided to continue as he fell, and slammed against a huge boulder that he had just ascended. Suspended from his climbing rope, he spotted a hiker below, shouted for help, and was rescued with just a few minor scrapes and bruises.

What is pride & rebellion?

Pride

Pride is a feeling of deep pleasure or satisfaction derived from one's achievements, the achievements of those with whom one is closely associated, or from one's qualities or possessions.

Rebellion

Rebellion is an act of violent or open resistance to an established government or ruler.

There is such a thing as good pride! Without being "prideful," we can be proud of our accomplishments. Like being proud of what we do in our place of work, we can be proud of our families as we together and individually meet our set goals. We can also be proud of our sons and daughters as they excel in school with academic projects and or in sports. Fathers can have pride as they walk their daughter down the aisle to give them away in marriage or the mother as she sees her daughter or son get married.

There is also pride that is not good, and as you continue to read this chapter, you will see some examples and stories explaining foolish pride.

> *1 Now the serpent was more crafty than any of the wild animals the LORD God had made. He said to the woman, "Did God really say, 'You must not eat from any tree in the garden'?"*
>
> *2 The woman said to the serpent, "We may eat fruit from the trees in the garden,*
>
> *3 but God did say, 'You must not eat fruit from the tree that is in the middle of the garden, and you must not touch it, or you will die.' " 4 "You will not certainly die," the serpent said to the woman.*
>
> *5 "For God knows that when you eat from it your eyes will be opened, and you will be like God, knowing good and evil." 6 When the woman saw that the fruit of the tree was good for food and pleasing to the eye, and also desirable for gaining wisdom, she took some and ate it. She also gave some to her husband, who was with her, and he ate it.*

7 Then the eyes of both of them were opened, and they realized they were naked; so they sewed fig leaves together and made coverings for themselves. 8 Then the man and his wife heard the sound of the LORD God as he was walking in the garden in the cool of the day, and they hid from the LORD God among the trees of the garden. 9 But the LORD God called to the man, "Where are you? (Genesis 3:1-9).

In their hearts, humans plan their course, but the LORD establishes their steps (Proverbs 16:9).

Pride goes before destruction, a haughty spirit before a fall (Proverbs 16:18).

As a child, a Blind Spot of Pride & Rebellion entered my life.

As a young man, I grew up in Washington State and enjoyed watching Tarzan on TV. As a 10-year-old boy, I was intrigued by the way Tarzan lived in the jungle, swinging from tree to tree by its vines. However, what interested me the most was how he whittled and carved branches to use as a spear to provide fish from the rivers to eat. I admired how Tarzan seemed so courageous, strong and wise, too.

One day while sitting and talking with Uncle Jim on my mother's side, I began to tell him how I admired Tarzan, and that I wanted a knife like Tarzan had so I could carve sticks to make spears. Uncle Jim chuckled at the way I asked for a knife, but because he had lots of money from a large inheritance, he said he would mention our conversation to my dad.

A week later, Uncle Jim discussed with my dad and let him know of our conversation about a knife and asked if he could purchase one for me. My dad said "yes," but only a folding pocketknife, not a large knife like Tarzan carried. I was permitted to only use the knife in the presence of an adult.

Uncle Jim took me to a local Western shop to purchase my brand-new pocketknife. I was super excited. My new knife, with it's bright white bone handle, fit perfectly in my right front blue jean pocket.

Approximately two weeks after receiving the knife as a gift from Uncle Jim, I asked my dad if I could use my knife to carve a stick. He said to be patient and wait so he could be with me.

I grew impatient. Later, when no one was home but me, I snuck into my parent's room to see where dad had hidden my knife. Once I found it, I left it in its place.

It seemed like my dad knew I had found it. On a Saturday afternoon, as he sat on one of our wooden chairs on the back porch reading the newspaper, he pulled my knife out of his jeans pocket. He handed it to me, along with a stick to carve on.

The next morning dad, mom, and my two sisters went to town to go grocery shopping. My brother Barry and I were the only ones at home. As he watched television in the living room, I snuck into my parent's bedroom to get my knife. I slipped it into my right front jeans pocket and headed to the backyard.

With my knife in hand, I hid behind a huge chestnut tree. The diameter of the tree's trunk was large enough that if anyone entered the backyard, they would not be able to view my disobedient act of rebellion. Since I had the new pocketknife Uncle Jim gave me in my hand, all I needed was a small branch on which to carve. At the base of our fence which bordered our neighbor's backyard, I eyed a small tree limb for my proposed project.

As I carved on the branch hiding behind the giant tree, I began to contemplate how much trouble I would be in if I had gotten caught. After all, I wasn't supposed to have or use my folding pocketknife without adult supervision.

I finished carving the branch into a small stick as I formed a very sharp point on one end. I then got up and peered around the chestnut tree trunk to see if the coast was clear to put my knife back in my parent's room and also to look for a place to hide my whittled branch.

After returning my knife to my parents' room in their nightstand, I then went back to my bedroom to hide the sharp pointed stick between my mattress and the bed springs.

After school the following day, I saw a man driving a dump truck and working at the end of our street. Saturday morning came, and that dump truck was sitting at the end of the road, but now it was unoccupied. As I kept my eyes focused on the empty dump truck, with no driver, I began fantasizing about what it would be like to be Tarzan in the jungle. My thoughts went back to one specific show in the Tarzan series. In this show, Tarzan had laid his knife horizontally across his mouth and dove off a large boulder into a river to fight an alligator that had been terrorizing a local village.

The next morning my dad, my brother Barry and I went fishing. It was barely light outside, but I could still see the dump truck as we drove past it on the way to the river. The fishing trip was mostly fun for me as I caught all the fish that day.

A full week had gone by, and each day I saw the man still in his dump truck working. Myself, along with several of my friends, sat on a sand pile across the street watching for hours as the dump truck was in full action, being loaded by a big machine and then dumping its contents on the site where they were working further up the street.

I got up early that Saturday morning, anticipating the dump truck would still be sitting in the same spot over the weekend again. I was super excited to see it was still there. I quickly ran back to my home. I went into my bedroom and lifted the edge of my mattress and grabbed the sharp pointed stick I had whittled and put it in my back pocket. Then I pulled my t-shirt over it to hide it from any of my family. I headed to the end of our street and finally found myself standing next to the dump truck I had admired so many times as I had passed each day for over a week. As I stood there looking up at the dump truck, I noticed the tires were taller than I was. The top of the dump bed seemed as if I was looking up at the height of the Seattle Space Needle. I began looking for a way to get up on the dump truck. I saw some welded stairs that workers must have used to climb onto this giant truck.

Just as Tarzan put his knife across his mouth to climb the large boulder, I put my whittled stick across my mouth and began to climb up the welded stairs on the dump truck that wrapped around to the opposite side of the dump truck bed. When I got to the top of the dump bed, I looked down and saw several tall piles of what looked like sand. I picked the highest one and jumped off the dump truck bed with my stick gripped by my teeth. Somehow, as I dropped, the pointed stick moved into my mouth. As I landed in a semi-crouched position, my jaw hit one of my knees, and the point of the stick lodged into the back of my mouth on my right-hand side between my teeth and my cheek. After rolling down the sand pile and on level ground, I got up and pulled the stick out of my mouth that had been lodged and began to taste my blood that was now running down my throat.

As I held the stick in my hand, I ran home and found my mom hanging clothes on a rope my father had suspended across two trees in our backyard. As my mom saw the stick in my hand and blood seeping from the corner of my mouth, she took me to the hose connected to our well water to rinse my mouth and inspect the damage from the pointed stick. The well water was so cold that it caused the area where the blood was coming from to clot rather quickly. Fortunately, I jumped onto a sand pile and not hard dirt. I also was very fortunate not to have broken any bones or to have been hurt much worse.

My restriction from fun activities was far worse than my physical hurt caused by my disobedience and rebellion. After my father got home, he took my shiny new folding pocketknife with the bright bone handle away from me and put it away for what seemed like an eternity to me.

As long as my family lived in that home, I would see the chestnut tree each time I was in the backyard and remember the wrong decision I made that day to carve the stick. The tree was not just the tree I had hidden behind in disobedience and rebellion; it was also one of the two trees that my dad suspended the rope from to hang laundry onto where I found my mom, who rescued me from the extreme action I caused.

Saul had everything going for him. Besides being the son of a highly respected man, he had good looks and a nice physique.

> *There was a Benjamite, a man of standing, whose name was Kish son of Abiel, the son of Zeror, the son of Bekorath, the son of Aphiah of Benjamin. 2 Kish had a son named Saul, as handsome a young man as could be found anywhere in Israel, and he was a head taller than anyone else* (1 Samuel 9:1-2).

Since God chose him to lead Israel at a time when the nation had some formidable enemies, we can surmise that he was also a courageous and charismatic leader.

> *Even the prophet Samuel was impressed and spoke admiringly at Saul's coronation: "Surely there is no one like him among all the people* (1 Samuel 10:24).

"Pride always drives a person away from God's path. With each misstep, an arrogant man or woman wanders farther into a spiritual wilderness. Nothing of lasting value can be found in such a desolate place. But the Lord will gladly welcome back the wayward. Blessing and joy await those who walk in step with Him." – **Dr. Charles Stanley.**

The Lord detests all the proud of heart.

> *Be sure of this: They will not go unpunished* (Proverbs 16:5).

> *In their hearts humans plan their course, but the Lord establishes their steps* (Proverbs 16:9).

> *Pride goes before destruction, a haughty spirit before a fall* (Proverbs 16:18).

The big question here is where did Pride & Rebellion begin?

For that answer, see Chapter 1 Where Did Blind Spots Originate?

Let's move onto a story that most Christians should know about concerning Pride & Rebellion

The fall in the Garden,

> *Now the serpent was more crafty than any of the wild animals the Lord God had made. He said to the woman, "Did God really say, 'You must not eat from any tree in the garden'?"*
>
> *2 The woman said to the serpent, "We may eat fruit from the trees in the garden, 3 but God did say, 'You must not eat fruit from the tree that is in the middle*

of the garden, and you must not touch it, or you will die.'"

4 *"You will not certainly die," the serpent said to the woman.* 5 *"For God knows that when you eat from it your eyes will be opened, and you will be like God, knowing good and evil."*

6 *When the woman saw that the fruit of the tree was good for food and pleasing to the eye, and also desirable for gaining wisdom, she took some and ate it. She also gave some to her husband, who was with her, and he ate it.* 7 *Then the eyes of both of them were opened, and they realized they were naked; so they sewed fig leaves together and made coverings for themselves.*

8 *Then the man and his wife heard the sound of the Lord God as he was walking in the garden in the cool of the day, and they hid from the Lord God among the trees of the garden.* 9 *But the Lord God called to the man, "Where are you?"*

10 *He answered, "I heard you in the garden, and I was afraid because I was naked; so I hid."*

11 *And he said, "Who told you that you were naked? Have you eaten from the tree that I commanded you not to eat from?"*

12 *The man said, "The woman you put here with me—she gave me some fruit from the tree, and I ate it."*

13 *Then the Lord God said to the woman, "What is this you have done?"*

The woman said, "The serpent deceived me, and I ate."

14 *So the Lord God said to the serpent, "Because you have done this,*

"Cursed are you above all livestock and all wild animals!

You will crawl on your belly and you will eat dust all the days of your life.

15 *And I will put enmity between you and the woman, and between your offspring[a] and hers; he will crush- your head, and you will strike his heel."*

16 *To the woman he said, "I will make your pains in childbearing very severe; with painful labor you will give birth to children. Your desire will be for your husband, and he will rule over you."*

17 *To Adam he said, "Because you listened to your wife and ate fruit from the tree about which I commanded you, 'You must not eat from it,' "Cursed is the ground because of you; through painful toil you will eat food from it all the days of your life.*

18 *It will produce thorns and thistles for you, and you will eat the plants of the field.*

19 *By the sweat of your brow you will eat your food until you return to the ground, since from it you were taken; for dust you are and to dust you will return"* (Genesis 3:1-9).

When pride comes, then comes disgrace, but with humility comes wisdom (Proverbs 11:2).

Questions to ponder and room to write as you leave this chapter!

How was this chapter helpful in my current circumstances?

_____
_____
_____
_____

What are the areas that I have unrighteous Pride?

_____
_____
_____
_____

What are the areas I walk in Rebellion?

_____
_____
_____
_____

What are my next steps to move towards freedom from Pride?

_____
_____
_____
_____

What are my next steps to move towards freedom from Rebellion?

_____
_____
_____
_____

God already knows your pain and wants to hear your voice so he can heal you emotionally, physically and spiritually!

Before entering the next chapter on Arrogance, please pause and pray this prayer:

Father God, thank you for highlighting and revealing my Blind Spot of Pride & Rebellion. I choose to exchange Pride & Rebellion for your obedience.

> *We demolish arguments and every pretension that sets itself up against the knowledge of God, and we take captive every thought to make it obedient to Christ* (2 Corinthians 10:5).

Lord, please remind me to read your Word as you open the door to take the proper steps to dissolve the damage done to my relationships.

Thank you, Holy Spirit for replacing rebellious thoughts with your words of truth.

Father God, I realize just reading this book is not enough for total healing, so I pray that you will place the right pastors, leaders, counselors, and friends who understand me to walk the rest of this healing journey with me.

I pray these things in Jesus name! Amen.

As you continue to read this book, I pray as you seek God that he will not only heal your past Pride & Rebellion, but he will help you in your present walk as you head into the future. Remember, God is always pursuing a deeper relationship with you.

Your new friend,

Pastor Mark

Part 4
Blind Spots That Can Destroy Relationships

Chapter 10
Arrogance

Don't confuse confidence with arrogance. Arrogance is being full of yourself, feeling you're always right, and believing your accomplishments or abilities make you better than other people. People often believe arrogance is excessive confidence, but it's really a lack of confidence. Arrogant people are insecure, and often repel others. Truly confident people feel good about themselves and attract others to them. – **CHRISTIE HARTMAN, It's Not Him, It's You**

What is arrogance?

Arrogance is an exaggerated sense of one's importance or abilities.

Here is a passage that illustrates God dealing with arrogance in the Old Testament

> Now the whole earth used the same language and the same words. 2 It came about as they journeyed east, that they found a plain in the land of Shinar and settled there. 3 They said to one another, "Come, let us make bricks and burn them thoroughly." And they used brick for stone, and they used tar for mortar. 4 They said, "Come, let us build for ourselves a city, and a tower whose top will reach into heaven, and let us make for ourselves a name, otherwise we will be scattered abroad over the face of the whole

> *earth." 5 The LORD came down to see the city and the tower which the sons of men had built. 6 The LORD said, "Behold, they are one people, and they all have the same language. And this is what they began to do, and now nothing which they purpose to do will be impossible for them. 7 "Come, let Us go down and there confuse their language, so that they will not understand one another's speech." 8 So the LORD scattered them abroad from there over the face of the whole earth; and they stopped building the city. 9 Therefore its name was called Babel, because there the LORD confused the language of the whole earth; and from there the LORD scattered them abroad over the face of the whole earth.* (Genesis 11:1-9)

So, as you just read in chapter 11, one large group of arrogant people at the TOWER OF BABEL were split and scattered into smaller groups of arrogant people.

If you decide to set this book down right now, take some time to read *Genesis* chapter 12 to see a sneak peek of how God chooses someone to help resolve one problem of arrogance.

Now, let's fast-forward to what looks like some more Babel in the Bible; OR IS IT?

> *When the day of Pentecost had come, they were all together in one place. 2 And suddenly there came from heaven a noise like a violent rushing wind, and it filled the whole house where they were sitting. 3 And there appeared to them tongues as of fire distributing themselves, and they rested on each one of them. 4 And they were all filled with the Holy Spirit*

and began to speak with other tongues, as the Spirit was giving them utterance.

5 Now there were Jews living in Jerusalem, devout men from every nation under heaven. 6And when this sound occurred, the crowd came together, and were bewildered because each one of them was hearing them speak in his own language. 7 They were amazed and astonished, saying, "Why, are not all these who are speaking Galileans? 8 "And how is it that we each hear them in our own language to which we were born? 9 "Parthians and Medes and Elamites, and residents of Mesopotamia, Judea and Cappadocia, Pontus and Asia, 10 Phrygia and Pamphylia, Egypt and the districts of Libya around Cyrene, and visitors from Rome, both Jews and proselytes, 11 Cretans and Arabs—we hear them in our own tongues speaking of the mighty deeds of God." 12 And they all continued in amazement and great perplexity, saying to one another, "What does this mean?" 13 But others were mocking and saying, "They are full of sweet wine" (Acts 2:1-12).

Peter's Sermon,

14 But Peter, taking his stand with the eleven, raised his voice and declared to them: "Men of Judea and all you who live in Jerusalem, let this be known to you and give heed to my words. 15 "For these men are not drunk, as you suppose, for it is only the third hour of the day; 16 but this is what was spoken of through the prophet Joel (Acts 2:1-16).

Arrogance led to Babel and Humbleness led to Communion/Communication with God.

After reading the passage in *Genesis* 11:1-9 above, it is plain to see that there is nothing new under the sun, and the fact is, arrogance has been around for a long time.

Pride & Rebellion at the Tower of Babel led to a vast group of arrogant people that said they didn't need God or want HIS direction and guidance anymore. So, they were scattered all over the face of the earth to become lots of smaller groups of arrogant people. This action led to 400 years of silence from God at the close of the Old Testament and the beginning of the New Testament. (See Chapter 10.)

Due to the arrogant attitude of the people building the Tower of Babel in the Old Testament, two-way communication with God and man and man and God was severed, just as it had been with Adam and Eve in the Garden of Eden; and wasn't restored until the Day of Pentecost, in Acts 2.

They rejected God's guidance, and the vertical from God to man and man to God was shut down by God himself, which then led to God shutting down the horizontal relationship of communication between humans to work together and construct the Tower of Babel.

As a young man, I had a Blind Spot of Arrogance in my life. Even though I wanted to be married and have an incredible loving marriage like my parents had, I wasn't married until I turned 40 years old.

However, all through high school and into adulthood, I considered myself to be God's gift to women. I hardly ever passed by a mirror without checking my looks, hair, etc., so I would look attractive to women. I felt like everyone ought to notice me when I walked into a room. I had become what was called a legend in my own my mind.

It wasn't until much later in life after becoming a prodigal son at the age of 40 that God began to speak through others for me to see my Blind Spot of Arrogance and how it had held me back from what I later encountered as God's plans and purposes for my life.

When I was 22 years of age, before I returned to my walk with Christ, I managed a construction company in El Cajon, California. I hired a young man named Rick who was a senior in high school at the time, and I trained him in several aspects of the construction field, so he could work part-time after school and on the weekends for our company.

After graduating high school, Rick had worked full-time for me for several years and seemed to have plateaued in his skills. I had a long daily meeting in the office with the owner, and one of the subjects during that meeting was to discuss Rick's abilities and skills. During the meeting, I decided to let him go. I had fully expected Rick to be just as good and fast at the skills as I was and many others that were on the labor payroll.

In my Blind Spot of Arrogance, I missed all of Rick's attributes; he was never late to work; in fact, he was always at least a half hour early, he respected authority, he cared about his work ethics and communicated well with me, the owner, co-workers, and customers on job sites too.

Four days after firing Rick, I realized he was much more of an asset to our company than a liability, so I called him, apologized for my arrogance and asked him if he would come back to work for me. To my surprise, Rick said yes and not only came back but within months his skills and speed increased, and I made him a foreman of one of our company crews.

You may wonder if I recognized my Blind Spot of Arrogance enough to get rid of it? I wish I could say yes! But I can't, but what I can say is that God had begun to give me a glimpse of the destruction that was causing relational collisions.

Here is a prophetic word from Jesus for his followers, both then and today. *But you will receive power when the Holy Spirit comes on you; and you will be my witnesses in Jerusalem, and in all Judea and Samaria, and to the ends of the earth* (Acts 1:8).

In Acts 2, as those who waited in the upper room were filled with His Holy Spirit, the communication between God and man was restored, and they were empowered to be His witnesses.

Many people are enamored with the appearance of tongues of fire, which was a sign of God's presence. All signs point to something. The Law points to Jesus Christ, tongues point to the communication between God and man, wholly restored.

Has a Blind Spot of Arrogance crept into your life and caused a block in communication between you, God and others? If so, God can heal that communication.

Questions to ponder and room to write as you leave this chapter!

How was this chapter helpful in my current circumstances?

_____
_____
_____
_____

How do I display Arrogance?

_____
_____
_____
_____

Who am I ignoring that has pointed out my Arrogance?

_____
_____

What are my next steps to move towards freedom from Arrogance?

___

Before entering the next chapter on Anger & Control, please pause and pray this prayer:

Father God, thank you for highlighting and revealing my Blind Spot of Arrogance. I choose to exchange Arrogance for a clean and pure heart.

> *Create in me a clean heart, O God; and renew a right spirit within me* (Psalm 51:10, KJV).

As I continue to walk out my journey in healing with You, I surrender my life, and I receive peace again.

> *And the peace of God, which transcends all understanding, will guard your hearts and your minds in Christ Jesus* (Philippians 4:7).

Father God, I realize just reading this book is not enough for total healing, so I pray that you will place the right pastors, leaders, counselors, and friends who understand me to walk the rest of this healing journey with me.

I pray these things in Jesus name! Amen.

God invites us to come to Him 24/7 with any of our life issues. He knows our pain and wants to hear our voices, so He can heal us emotionally, physically, and spiritually!

I pray as you seek God in this, that he will not only heal your past, but he will help you in your present heading into the future. Remember, God is always pursuing and deepening his relationship with you.

Your new friend,

Pastor Mark

Chapter 11
Anger & Control

God is large and in charge, which means,
God is in Control!

What is anger & control?

Anger is a strong feeling of annoyance, displeasure, or hostility.

Control is the power to influence or direct another's behavior or the course of events.

Two questions:

- What happens when you take control and push God out of the way? Where does unrighteous control lead us?

- What occurs when your anger takes over Gods position? Where does anger lead us?

What if I said, Control to get our way can lead to anger!

Why do I say this? Think of a child that is throwing a temper tantrum. In other words, wanting what they can't have that leads to acting out in anger!

Adults often act out in anger due to childhood experiences as they threw temper tantrums to control particular situations. But what happens when a Blind Spot of Anger & Control creeps into childhood and continues into adulthood?

In the first year of marriage, my wife, my father-in-law and other family members attempted to point out a Blind Spot in my life.

However, due to my already having a Blind Spot of Pride, I couldn't see Blind Spots of Anger & Control that I also carried. Sadly, it was easily seen by those I loved, especially my wife. (See Pride & Rebellion Chapter 9.)

The following is a sad story of a generational Blind Spot of Anger & Control.

In the Bible, The Herod family dynasty was a perfect example of the powers of darkness.

Herod the Great had all children in Bethlehem, two years old and younger, put to death. He was attempting to kill Jesus. His son, Herod Antipas had John the Baptist beheaded, which led to the Herod dynasty of those powers of darkness continuing in Acts Chapter 12 with Herod the Great's grandson, King Herod Agrippa. In Acts Chapter 12, to gain favor with the Jews, the Roman king Agrippa arrested James the brother of John, and had him killed by the sword.

Acts chapter 12 starting in verse 1-4,

> *It was about this time that King Herod arrested some who belonged to the church, intending to persecute them. 2 He had James, the brother of John, put to death with the sword. 3 When he saw that this met with approval among the Jews, he proceeded to seize Peter also. It happened during the Festival of Unleavened Bread. 4 After arresting him, he put him in prison, handing him over to be guarded by four squads of four soldiers each. Herod intended to bring him out for public trial after the Passover.*

To keep all the religious sects happy, the King honored Jewish Laws and events and the Jewish event at that time was Feast of unleavened bread, which followed the Passover. So, Peter is put in prison rather than executed. The King then ordered 16 soldiers to guard him.

Peter was arrested for the third time. Why were 16 soldiers assigned to guard Peter? Apparently, King Agrippa had heard about the soldier's who had guarded Jesus' tomb when the stone was rolled away.

In Matthew's gospel, we read that not one guard at Jesus tomb was put to death for Jesus body missing. There was a story told that his disciples came and stole the body while the guards were asleep.

> *While the women were on their way, some of the guards went into the city and reported to the chief priests everything that had happened. 12 When the chief priests had met with the elders and devised a plan, they gave the soldiers a large sum of money, 13 telling them, "You are to say, 'His disciples came during the night and stole him away while we were asleep.' 14 If this report gets to the governor, we will satisfy him and keep you out of trouble." 15 So the soldiers took the money and did as they were instructed. And this story has been widely circulated among the Jews to this very day* (Matthew 28:11-15).

So, Peter was kept in prison, but the church was earnestly praying to God for him (Acts 12:5).

The word earnestly in verse 5 is the same Greek word in Luke 22:44 that Jesus uses in the Garden of Gethsemane, which means to contend for (literally, to "struggle upon, appropriately") with skill and commitment in opposing whatever is not of faith.

As the church body remembers the terrible execution of James, The Holy Spirit brings the church together to pray for Peter, who was suffering in prison, and to plead for his very life.

What happens when we earnestly pray? God moves on our behalf!

The temptation is not a sin; however, when we don't control our anger, it becomes a sin. The Bible says,

> *In your anger do not sin" Do not let the sun go down while you are still angry* (Ephesians 4:26).

We need to learn to channel our anger into righteous anger, so that it doesn't control us, or cause us to want to control another person(s) or circumstance(s) in a harmful way.

We find the nine fruit of the Holy Spirit in Galatians Chapter 5. They are the nine attributes of a person or community filled with the Holy Spirit.

> *But the fruit of the Spirit is love, joy, peace, patience, kindness, goodness, faithfulness, gentleness, and self-control. The tongue and bring death or life; those who love to talk will reap the consequences* (Galatians 5:22-23).

Self-control begins with holding our tongue!

> *The tongue can bring death or life; those who love to talk will reap the consequences* (Proverbs 18:21, NLT).

Earlier, in *A Personal Note From The Author*, I said that by the time I had turned 40 and had not yet married, discovered that my #1 Blind Spot at the time was Pride & Rebellion. At that time, not only did I not realize people can have Blind Spot(s), but due to my selfish pride, I was not aware of my own.

The Lord reminds us of this in *Matthew 7:5,*

You hypocrite, first take the plank out of your eye, and then you will see clearly to remove the speck from your brother's eye.

Questions to ponder and room to write as you leave this chapter!

How was this chapter helpful in my current circumstances?

_____
_____
_____
_____

What causes my unrighteous Anger?

_____
_____
_____
_____

What and/or who do I try to Control?

_____
_____
_____
_____

What are my next steps to move towards freedom from unrighteous Anger?

_____
_____
_____
_____

What are my next steps to move towards freedom from Control?

_____
_____
_____
_____

Before entering the next chapter on Temptation, please pause and pray this prayer:

Father God, thank you for highlighting and revealing my Blind Spot of Anger & Control.

As I continue to walk out my journey in healing with you, please help me to read your word as you open the door to take steps to dissolve the damage done to my relationships, and not to fear all of that stuff on my mind right now. I give it to you God, and I receive peace again.

Holy Spirit, thank you for replacing those Anger & Control thoughts with your words of truth.

> *My dear brothers and sisters, take note of this: Everyone should be quick to listen, slow to speak and slow to become angry,* [20] *because human anger does not produce the righteousness that God desires* (James 1:19-20).

You know what concerns me; I choose to guard my heart, and not to allow Anger & Control to guide my life anymore.

Father God, I realize just reading this book is not enough for total healing, so I pray that you will place the right pastors, leaders, counselors, and friends who understand me to walk the rest of this healing journey with me.

I pray these things in Jesus name! Amen.

I pray as you seek God in this, that he will not only heal your past, but he will help you in your present heading into the future. Remember, God is always pursuing and deepening his relationship with you.

Your new friend,

Pastor Mark

Chapter 12
Temptation

During the gestation period of temptation, there are usually 100's and 100's of contemplative thoughts before it births. That's why, as a pastor, I like to say,

> "We don't *fall* into sin; we *slip* into it slowly"
> — **Pastor Mark Baxter**

What is temptation?

Temptation is a desire to do something, especially wrong or unwise; or a thing or course of action that attracts or tempts someone. Let me start with this statement: Temptation in and of itself is not a sin!

The Greek word for temptation is *peirazo*, which means to tempt or to test in a negative sense.

> *When tempted, no one should say, "God is tempting me." For God cannot be tempted by evil, nor does he tempt anyone; 14 but each person is tempted when they are dragged away by their own evil desire and enticed. 15 Then, after desire has conceived, it gives birth to sin; and sin, when it is full-grown, gives birth to death* (James 1:13-15).

The *death* referred to in the Scripture above, refers to spiritual death, which means separation from God, not physical death. We know this because the narrative later states that Adam and Eve (still physically alive) were expelled from the Garden of Eden to never return to it.

God cares and loves us so much that he always provides a way of escape from sin that is creeping at the door of our heart.

> *No temptation has overtaken you except what is common to mankind. And God is faithful; he will not let you be tempted beyond what you can bear. But when you are tempted] he will also provide a way out so that you can endure it* (1 Corinthians 10:13).

As you read in the first chapter, *Where Did Blind Spots Originate,* you saw that Blind Spots didn't begin with Adam and Eve, but when Satan made the irreversible/irreparable decision to think he could be equal to God.

So, if Lucifer, one of the angels God created, could have a Blind Spot, then why wouldn't we think we would have them as well?

It certainly appears temptation was in the Garden of Eden even before Satan tempted Eve. Why do I say this?

Nowhere does the Bible say that God told Eve not to eat the fruit of, or to touch the tree of the knowledge of good and evil.

However, God did speak to and tell Adam the Do's and Don'ts in the Garden!

If Adam was to share that same information God shared with him about the tree of the knowledge of good and evil with his wife Eve; we know how men and women communicate at times. The Scripture doesn't say it, but we must assume that Adam would have shared such essential knowledge with his wife, Eve. But then we must also ask ourselves why would the serpent have gone to Eve to tempt her first?

Remember, both Adam and Eve were standing at the forbidden tree when the serpent appeared!

Some other questions to ponder that the Bible doesn't answer!

- Did Adam adequately explain to Eve about the tree of the knowledge of good and evil?
- What was Adam doing while the serpent was tempting his wife?
- Was he staring at all the animals he had named?
- Was he waiting to see if physical death would occur when Eve ate the fruit?
- When Eve ate the fruit and Adam saw that she didn't die, did Adam think that God was holding out on him?

One thing we know for sure, is what God said to Adam.

> *The Lord God took the man and put him in the Garden of Eden to work it and take care of it. 16 And the Lord God commanded the man, "You are free to eat from any tree in the garden; 17 but you must not eat from the tree of the knowledge of good and evil, for when you eat from it you will certainly die* (Genesis 2:15-17).

Satan began tempting people in the Garden of Eden. Years later, he tempted Jesus at one of his weakest moments, after he had fasted 40 days and nights in the desert. *Jesus battled Satan with the Word of God.*

Jesus was tempted in every way that you and I are tempted. Satan tempted Jesus in the desert, immediately after his water baptism and his baptism in the Holy Spirit. Jesus then combatted the temptation with truth from Scripture, which Satan twisted.

Jesus answered,

> *It is written: 'Man shall not live on bread alone, but on every word that comes from the mouth of God* (Matthew 4:4).

Where does Jesus pull this verse from in *Matthew* 4:4? He recalls it from the Old Testament,

> *He humbled you, causing you to hunger and then feeding you with manna, which neither you nor your ancestors had known, to teach you that man does not live on bread alone but on every word that comes from the mouth of the LORD* (Deuteronomy 8:3).

Jesus answered him,

> *It is also written: 'Do not put the Lord your God to the test* (Matthew 4:7).

Where does Jesus pull this verse from in Matthew 4:7? He recalls it from the Old Testament,

> *Do not put the LORD your God to the test as you did at Massah* (Deuteronomy 6:16).

Jesus said to him,

> *Away from me, Satan! For it is written: 'Worship the Lord your God, and serve him only* (Matthew 4:10).

Where does Jesus pull this verse from in Matthew 4:10? He recalls it from the Old Testament

> *Fear the LORD your God, serve him only and take your oaths in his name* (Deuteronomy 6:13).

In the Garden of Eden, we discovered Adam and Eve's Blind Spots. In Matthew Chapter 4, we find that Satan has his own Blind Spots.

- Satan's first Blind Spot was the Pride of wanting to be like God. For that, he was cast out of heaven.
- There we learn that the same power of God that cast Satan from heaven, operated through Jesus as He defeated Satan in the desert… God's Word!

Questions to ponder and room to write as you leave this chapter!

How was this chapter helpful in my current circumstances?

_____
_____
_____
_____

When do I feel Temptation?

_____
_____
_____
_____

How do I avoid Temptation?

_____
_____
_____
_____

What are my next steps to move towards freedom when Temptation knocks on my door?

_____
_____
_____
_____

Before entering the next chapter on Lust, please pause and pray this prayer:

Father God, thank you for highlighting and revealing my Blind Spot of Temptation. I choose to exchange my Blind Spot of Temptation for obedience to follow Your commands.

As I learn to walk this journey in healing with you, will You constantly remind me that the Bible is the authoritative Word of God.

I know you go before me, and you have my back as I travel this journey through discovering all my Blind Spots that have destroyed relationships in my life.

Father God, I realize just reading this book is not enough for total healing, so I pray that you will place the right pastors, leaders, counselors, and friends who understand me to walk the rest of this healing journey with me.

I pray these things in Jesus name! Amen.

Your new friend,

Pastor Mark

Chapter 13
Lust

Lust is like an ice cream sandwich on steroids! Both types of lust are the outside cookie parts, and the pleasure of the lust itself being the ice cream in between.

What is lust?

Sexual lust is an intense or unbridled sexual desire.

Worldly lust is to crave things that are only temporal.

When I was seven-years-old, and my brother Barry was eight, an elderly single man named Albert Summers II lived way behind our home on a couple of acres of his land. When my brother Barry and I played army at the far end of our backyard, we would see Mr. Summers wave at us. He would say hi as my brother, and I would do the same back to him.

My parents didn't know Mr. Summers or anything about him, so we weren't able to spend any time with him at all. Approximately three months after we moved in next to Mr. Summers, Barry and I noticed that we hadn't seen him out in his yard for a couple of weeks. We heard from our childhood friends that lived on the acreage on the other side of Mr. Summers that he had passed away and had no relatives to leave his home and belongings to; so his house and property just sat there abandoned.

My brother and I now knew that no one was on the late Mr. Summers property, we immediately began an adventure as we dug a shallow hole just deep enough to skinny our way beneath our backyard fence to check out his property. Barry and I didn't enter the home, but we explored the property. We found lots of cool stuff like a pile of long pieces of old lumber, along with some old warped plywood. His property was mostly dirt with very little grass. So, Barry and I began to drag pieces of lumber and plywood from the massive pile to the area we had targeted to build our fort.

We planned to dig the hole, and to line the walls with the long lumber. We would use some of the plywood as makeshift walls to keep the dirt from caving in on us when we were inside. Also, we would use one piece of plywood as the roof and cover it with a slight amount of dirt to hide it from my parents, my other siblings, or any other onlookers.

We began to dig with the same shovel with which we dug the hole under our fence to climb through to Mr. Summer's property. As we dug down about two feet, we hit something that made a big thud sound. We tried digging in different areas, but the same thud sound occurred again and again throughout the diameter of the hole we drew out in the soft dirt with the shovel handle. We got excited thinking we had discovered some buried treasure that Mr. Summers, or perhaps a previous owner had hidden.

We set the shovel down, so we didn't damage our so-called treasure. We carefully moved the rest of the dirt by hand. When we finally opened the "treasure chest," we discovered it held no treasure. Instead, it was filled with old magazines.

As Barry and I opened them, we looked at each other shocked by what we saw. They were porn magazines, filled with pictures of completely nude women in many different poses. It seemed like we sat there looking at the magazines for hours, but it was only a few minutes.

I told Barry that before we got caught, that we needed to throw the magazines back in the hole and bury it. We did just that and headed for home as we filled back in the shallow hole beneath our fence and never returned to Mr. Summer's property again.

The problem wasn't that we found the X-rated magazines; it was that the nude photos were now etched in our minds. We were too young to know the damage done by our having seen something that was forbidden.

Even though I was clueless, a Blind Spot of Lust entered my life that day, that would haunt me for many years to come.

Once Satan set his demonic hook of porn magazines in my life at seven years of age, he began bringing temptation through my friend's older brothers. They had porn magazines that were not hidden well enough from us. Even as a young grade-schooler, I was enticed by sexual desires, that are only intended for a husband and wife.

I also seemed to make friends with those who were like-minded at school. Between the magazines, and me trying to sneak a peek at my friend's junior high and high school sisters through the skeleton keyhole in their bedroom doors, I was on a destructive path of sexual sin through a Blind Spot of Lust.

Not being married until I was 40 years old, and walking away from Jesus more than seventeen years, I led a very promiscuous lifestyle, along with prescription drugs, street drugs, and alcohol along with frequenting bars weekly. The fetish for magazines wasn't enough anymore as I started going to strip clubs on a regular basis, which began after my first time in a strip club for a friend's bachelor party.

Most of my friends were married, and I regret helping several of them keep a secret from their wives of going to a strip club. My biggest regret at that time was that one of my best friends and his wife divorced due to his becoming addicted to porn and strip clubs.

I began having recurring radical, destructive dreams of me being in horrible earthquakes, floods, hurricanes, and tornados, which depicted my lifestyle. The more sex I had, the more drugs I took, and the more alcohol I drank, the more my destructive dreams intensified. I began to take a serious look at my life. My head was so cloudy from my ungodly lifestyle that I couldn't see God was drawing me back to my first love/Jesus.

In 2005, I entered some inner healing prayer called *theophostic*, Greek for God's light. I went in for healing prayer to deal with an anger problem. However, God, as He often does, had different plans that day. I've seen that through the years as I've ministered to others.

In that Theophostic meeting, God took me back to that very day when I was only seven years old at the hole in the ground. God showed me Jesus standing there, pouring gasoline over the magazines and pointing his index finger. Suddenly, all the magazines got torched as they burned to just soot and stuck to the inner sides of the dirt hole.

In that Theophostic inner healing meeting, God revealed my Blind Spot of Lust and gently asked me if I wanted my innocence restored. Before I could say yes, Jesus, knowing my thoughts, torched all the magazines so His power could destroy the tormenting hold that Satan had tattooed on my mind and heart all those years earlier.

I was grateful to be free from the load I had carried so long. I could look at women as God's creation, rather than objects created for my pleasure.

The Bible mentions two types of lust.

> *Do not love the world or anything in the world. If anyone loves the world, love for the Father is not in them. 16 For everything in the world—the lust of the flesh, the lust of the eyes, and the pride of life—comes not from the Father but from the world. 17 The world and its desires pass away, but whoever does the will of God lives forever* (1 John 2:15-17).

- Lust of the eyes

Adam and Eve encountered lust as their legitimate needs are met illegitimately at the tree of the knowledge of good and evil. In the narrative in the book of Genesis, something from Adam and Eve had surmised that God was holding something back from them that they would want, but what God was doing is teaching them obedience. More than that, God was protecting them from something that would harm their future.

We, also as humans like Adam and Eve, tend to follow the same path, depending on our ways to fulfill desires.

- Lust of the flesh

Paul says this about the lust of the flesh,

The acts of the flesh are obvious: sexual immorality, impurity and debauchery; 20 idolatry and witchcraft; hatred, discord, jealousy, fits of rage, selfish ambition, dissensions, factions 21 and envy; drunkenness, orgies, and the like. I warn you, as I did before, that those who live like this will not inherit the kingdom of God (Galatians 5:19-21).

Lust is like an ice cream sandwich on steroids. Internet porn is like a pornography magazine on steroids! Internet porn runs rampant in many men today, both Christian and non-Christian. The difference is, magazines can be easily exposed, whereas Internet porn can be hidden or deleted on one's phone, computer, or tablet.

When men try to find significance and pleasure in porn, they end up running into a massive problem of control in their life. (See Anger & Control Chapter 11.)

Pornography delivers half-truths through Satan. He whispers how it will bring pleasure and fulfill our immediate sexual desires. Even though true, Satan doesn't tell you about the shame and guilt that it brings as he accuses you after you meet that desire. Only you, God and Satan are the ones that see it. Sometimes this sin is revealed through an addiction to drugs or alcohol or both trying to cover the pain of shame and guilt. (See Shame Chapter 2; and Guilt Chapter 3.)

When men look at porn magazines, Internet-porn or go to strip clubs, then close their eyes to make love to their wives, they mentally see the other woman.

How often do we hear the word "coveting?" After all, "*you shall not covet*" was the 10th commandment that God gave to the Israelites.

The sin of coveting is a prime example of the result of giving in to the lust of the eyes.

Let's face it; there is nothing wrong with looking at beautiful things. There are many beautiful paintings, statues and even creation itself is breathtaking. Is there anything more beautiful than a rainbow, a mountain landscape, the ocean or stars? Also looking at beautiful women or handsome men is allowed in the right context, as recognized as part of God's creation.

However, when we find ourselves lustfully looking upon things God has commanded us to avoid, such as pornography, other people's spouses, or other people's possessions, it becomes sin.

What is coveting? To covet means to have a yearning or a strong desire to have something that rightfully belongs to someone else.

One example was Satan wanting to be like God

> You said in your heart,
> "I will ascend to the heavens;
> I will raise my throne
> above the stars of God;
> I will sit enthroned on the mount of assembly,
> on the utmost heights of Mount Zaphon.
> 14 I will ascend above the tops of the clouds;
> I will make myself like the Most High." 15 But you are brought down to the realm of the dead,
> to the depths of the pit (Isaiah 14:13-15).

The temptation is not a sin! We are born into a sin nature from what Adam & Eve did in the Garden, and we all sin every day, but it becomes a sin when we chase the temptation.

LUST

The narrative in 2 Samuel 20:1-27 shares both types of lust:

That's not fair that he has such a beautiful wife. I want her as my wife, is a prime example.

> *In the spring, at the time when kings go off to war, David sent Joab out with the king's men and the whole Israelite army. They destroyed the Ammonites and besieged Rabbah. But David remained in Jerusalem. 2 One evening David got up from his bed and walked around on the roof of the palace. From the roof he saw a woman bathing. The woman was very beautiful, 3 and David sent someone to find out about her. The man said, "She is Bathsheba, the daughter of Eliam and the wife of Uriah the Hittite."*

4 Then David sent messengers to get her. She came to him, and he slept with her. (Now she was purifying herself from her monthly uncleanness.) Then she went back home. 5 The woman conceived and sent word to David, saying, "I am pregnant." 6 So David sent this word to Joab: "Send me Uriah the Hittite." And Joab sent him to David. 7 When Uriah came to him, David asked him how Joab was, how the soldiers were and how the war was going. 8 Then David said to Uriah, "Go down to your house and wash your feet." So Uriah left the palace, and a gift from the king was sent after him. 9 But Uriah slept at the entrance to the palace with all his master's servants and did not go down to his house. 10 David was told, "Uriah did not go home." So he asked Uriah, "Haven't you just come from a military campaign? Why didn't you go home?" 11 Uriah said to David, "The ark and Israel and Judah are staying in tents, and my commander Joab and my lord's men are camped in the open country. How could I go to my house to eat and drink and make love to my wife? As surely as you live, I will not do such a thing!" 12 Then David said to him, "Stay here one more day, and tomorrow I will send you back." So Uriah remained in Jerusalem that day and the next. 13 At David's invitation, he ate and drank with him, and David made him drunk. But in the evening Uriah went out to sleep on his mat among his master's servants; he did not go home. 14 In the morning David wrote a letter to Joab and sent it with Uriah. 15 In it he wrote, "Put Uriah out in front where the fighting is fiercest. Then withdraw from him so he will be struck down and die." 16 So while Joab had the city under siege, he put Uriah at a place where he knew the strongest defenders were. 17 When the men of the city came out and fought against Joab, some of the men in David's army fell; moreover, Uriah the Hittite died. 18 Joab sent David a full account of the battle. 19 He instructed the messenger: "When you have finished giving the king this account of the battle, 20 the king's anger may flare up, and he may ask you, 'Why did you get so close to the city to fight? Didn't you know they would shoot arrows from the wall? 21 Who killed Abimelek son of Jerub-Besheth[b]? Didn't a woman drop an upper millstone on him from the wall, so that he died in Thebez? Why did you get so close to the wall?' If he asks you this, then say to him, 'Moreover, your servant Uriah the Hittite is dead.'" 22 The messenger set out, and when he arrived he told David everything Joab had sent him to say. 23 The messenger said to David, "The men overpowered us and came out against us in the open, but we drove them back to the entrance of the city gate. 24 Then the archers shot arrows at your servants from the wall, and some of the king's men died. Moreover, your servant Uriah the Hittite is dead." 25 David told the messenger, "Say this to Joab: 'Don't let this upset you; the sword devours one as well as another. Press the attack against the city and destroy it.' Say this to encourage Joab." 26 When Uriah's wife heard that her husband was dead, she mourned for him. 27 After the time of mourning was over, David had her brought to his house, and she became his wife and bore him a son. But the thing David had done displeased the Lord.

Did the Lord reveal a Blind Spot of Lust through your reading my childhood story, or King David's? Did He tug on your heart and reveal another Blind Spot(s) that you may have read earlier on in my book, but didn't feel pertinent to your life as you read it?

> *Then when lust hath conceived, it bringeth forth sin: and sin, when it is finished, bringeth forth death* (James 1:15, KJV).

If you feel like something is opening your heart up from a previous chapter(s) you read, pause now and go back and reread that chapter(s), then return to finish my book later.

Questions to ponder and room to write as you leave this chapter!

How was this chapter helpful in my current circumstances?

_____
_____
_____
_____

How do I recognize when I'm in Lust mode?

_____
_____
_____
_____

What are some of the areas of Lust I chase?

_____
_____
_____
_____

What are my next steps to move towards freedom from Lust?

_____
_____
_____
_____

Before entering the next chapter on Addiction, please pause and pray this prayer:

Father God, thank you for highlighting and revealing my Blind Spot of Lust. I choose to exchange Lust for the desires You have for me.

> *So I say, walk by the Spirit, and you will not gratify the desires of the flesh* (Galatians 5:16)

As I continue to walk out my journey in healing from Blind Spots, and I learn not to be in Lust, I desire to hear You and listen to what You say about Lust.

Father God, I realize just reading this book is not enough for total healing, so I pray that you will place the right pastors, leaders, counselors, and friends who understand me to walk the rest of this healing journey with me.

I pray these things in Jesus name! Amen.

Your new friend,

Pastor Mark

Chapter 14
Addiction

Although it was 50 years ago, I vividly remember how cold and numb my hands felt as I stood on the playground during morning recess at *Morgan Junior High School*, in Ellensburg, Washington. I was barehanded as I picked up snow to form a snowball that barely fit into both hands. I gently set it on the snow-covered playground and began rolling it until it was so large that I needed help to continue.

Some of my classmates saw how large the snowball was getting for me to handle and came alongside to help me. Right before the recess bell went off to return to class, we rolled the snowball to a height that we could no longer see past to continue. We were all super excited and couldn't wait to get back out on the playground for noon recess.

I watched the clock like an Eagle looking down from a mile up in the air, staring at a salmon below the surface of a calm area in a river for its next meal.

When we went back out for noon recess, the snowball and the ground were as one from the freezing weather. It took me, along with most of my classmates, to even budge the snowball. As the snowball began to roll again, it got so large and tall that even our PE coach, Mr. Christianson, a rather large, tall and robust man had to come over to help us push. And with every kid on the playground pushing with all our might, the snowball got to such an enormous size of almost six feet tall. Even though Mr. Christianson was helping push, too, we could no longer move it. The cold weather continued for several weeks as the nighttime temperature dropped to 30 degrees and kept the snowball frozen. The sun barely thawed it during the day. So, that crazy and fun, large snowball remained in the same spot on the playground until the sun finally melted it, which took close to a month due to the cold winter. Very few of us had on warm or waterproof gloves or mittens! So, we were all freezing, but we all felt accomplished.

One thing still sticks in my mind about that day, it was how loud the squeaking noise had gotten from every rotation of the snowball as it picked up the freshly fallen snow right down to the grass. It was fascinating to see the snowball grow. You see, it wasn't just snow that the snowball picked up that made it bigger, but it also picked up fallen branches from trees, broken sticks, rocks, pebbles, dirt and virtually anything and everything that was in its path as it rolled across the playground.

I shared my memorable childhood story about the nature of a snowball and how it grows for a specific purpose. Right now, as you read this, you may be asking, what does that story have to do with addiction, or how do we know if we have a Blind Spot of Addiction?

A Blind Spot of Addiction comes to life when you in your heart of hearts believe you have full control over what you say you are not addicted to in your life, even though others see that you are, as your path of destruction continues just like the snowball effect.

A snowball is the best analogy I have ever come up with for addiction, although I also have a metaphor I came up with that I like just as much, more on that later in this chapter.

Every addiction starts out small!

No one wakes up one morning and decides to be a career drug addict, alcoholic, porn addict, anorexic, bulimic, or any other life-controlling and destroying addiction.

Whether or not it is alcohol, marijuana, or another drug that an addict starts with, it just seems like there is always a way for the addict to succeed in achieving a more significant and better high.

However, it still leads to more destructive behavior as one-by-one, family and friends get dragged along for the ride!

As the snowball is icy and cold, so it is with an addict's heart toward God.

I don't say that as a result of a book I read about addictions, but from experiences I had early in my life.

As a pastor, I talk to a lot of people that are addicted to many different things. It's so funny how most try to persuade me; otherwise, that is until I share my testimonial of how God pulled me out of the pit of a hellish lifestyle I was leading for almost 17 1/2 years of excess alcohol, drugs, porn, etc.

My metaphor of addiction goes like this: it is merely a caged monster waiting for someone to come along to feed. In other words, we start small, like feeding the beast in the cage and then the Blind Spot of Addiction becomes the key for that monster to let itself out of the cage and chase us daily. That addiction that you thought you had control over now has power over you!

As I mentioned earlier on, a heart can be cold and icy towards God when stuck in addiction. The only way for it to melt is through Jesus by the power of the Holy Spirit, as Abba Father intimately loves on us!

Much like a snowball picks up sticks, pebbles, rocks and everything in the path, so does the snowball of addiction. The only difference in the two snowballs is the snowball of addiction has hands, feet, and heads sticking out of it, and those body parts represent all the enabling friends and especially family members being picked up as the snowball of addiction rolls on.

As I have experienced addiction, I have also experienced being set free by Jesus. Many addicts that I have talked to, as well as counseled with, believe they can stop there addictions on their own. However, that's incorrect. As a previous addict, I came to my senses and realized that doing it myself could only stop it temporarily.

When a major tragedy occurs, like the death of a family member, or automobile accident, an addict will revert to what was familiar to block the emotional pain!

Through my experience, as well as those I have been privileged to pastor through addiction, I have discovered there is only one way to be set free. That is to experience a surrendered relationship with Jesus Christ!

The way this process begins, if you haven't yet given the steering wheel of life to Jesus, you can do that right now and go after Jesus harder than you ever went after that which caused your addiction.

You might now be ready to let Jesus run your life—after all, he created you through two seeds.

How to give over your steering wheel of life to Jesus!

Father, I know that I'm a sinner in desperate need of a Savior.

I know that you died on the cross for my past, present and future sins!

Jesus, I receive you into my heart by faith right now. Lead me the rest of my life. You are my Lord.

Thank you for saving me! Amen

If you just prayed that prayer from your heart, you are born-again. Congrats to you, my new brother or sister in Christ!

Salvation is that simple. Now, get plugged into a local community of believers, a Bible-believing church, where you can grow in your faith.

Questions to ponder and room to write as you leave this chapter!

How was this chapter helpful in my current circumstances?

_____
_____
_____
_____

What is my closet Addiction(s)?

_____
_____
_____
_____

What people do I ignore that point out an Addiction in my life?

_____
_____
_____
_____

What are my next steps to move towards freedom from Addiction?

_____
_____
_____
_____

Before entering the next chapter on ministry, please pause and pray this prayer:

Father God, thank you for highlighting and revealing my Blind Spot of Addiction. I choose to exchange Addiction for your peace that surpasses all understanding.

And the peace of God, which transcends all understanding, will guard your hearts and your minds in Christ Jesus (Philippians 4:7).

As I continue to walk out my journey in healing with you, please help me to read your Word as you open the door to take the proper steps in dissolving the damage done to my relationships. As I learn not to be in Addiction, I release all the stuff on my mind right now. I give it to you God, and I receive your peace.

Thank you, Holy Spirit, for replacing those thoughts of Addiction with your words of truth. You know what concerns me! I choose this day to guard my heart, not to allow fear to control my life and to focus my mind on what truth is in the midst turmoil I may face because I know you go before me and you have my back.

Father God, I realize just reading this book is not enough for total healing, so I pray that you will place the right pastors, leaders, counselors, and friends who understand me to walk the rest of this healing journey with me.

I pray these things in Jesus name! Amen.

Your new friend,

Pastor Mark

Chapter 15
Ministry

You might wonder how ministry can become a Blind Spot.

I gave my life to Christ when I was 16-years-old at the San Diego Jack Murphy Stadium, but walked away four years later to pursue a life of destruction for seventeen and one-half years. I rededicated my life back to Jesus on February 4th, 1995 at 2:00 AM in the morning as a prodigal son. After returning to my first love, Jesus, in 1995, I began attending Foothills Christian Fellowship in El Cajon, California at 365 West Bradley Avenue, where Dave and Mark Hoffman co-pastor.

I got involved in a small group right away, where I later met my wife. I was young when Jesus found me lost in my little world. I was not aware at the time how important the community within the body of Christ would become. I also didn't know about fellowship and accountability to one another and just how important that was. I later found out that transparency is the best policy to keep the devil from beating you up when trying to confess about a closet sin; it brings the light, which is Jesus into the darkness. Therefore, breaking the power that the enemy takes over us when we give way to him in secret. At that time, I didn't understand the Holy Spirit, let alone the power of God.

After every Sunday service at FCF, the altar call came, and the Lord had been teaching me in my heart of hearts the real importance of being humble in all situations, if possible, and through Christ, it was starting to happen in my life.

I went forward for prayer at the altar for the first time and ended up not just getting great prayer, but also to my surprise. I got baptized in the Holy Spirit. My walk with Jesus changed dramatically, and I knew that I was for sure ruined for the kingdom of darkness. After that extraordinary experience with the Lord, every Sunday I went forward for prayer to find out what else God might want to give me. By the fifth or sixth Sunday in a row, I was up there at the altar each time, surrendering to God as he met me. One particular Sunday as I lay on the carpet, the Lord spoke to me and said these exact words to me: "I want you to let others receive what you have been receiving from me."

Long story short, I had a brief argument with God for about 45 minutes on the carpet. Every time I tried to get up off the floor, I felt like my body had glued to it. When I would try to open up my eyes, they would slam shut. Then the Lord said, "I want you to join the ministry team to become a prayer warrior for me." After I agreed to join, God let me up off the floor. Of course, on the way out of the church, I said, "I'm not going to do that."

The following Thursday night at small group, the home fellowship leader came up to me and said that the ministry team director at *Foothills Christian Fellowship* had called him along with every small group leader, asking each one of them who they felt would be ready to join the ministry team. Dan Deyling, my home fellowship leader, told his brother, Jim, the Ministry team director, that the person ready to join would be me.

The following week, I joined the team. Much to my surprise, God used me in a big way, as I became a hollow vessel for him. The Holy Spirit powerfully moved through me and healed some people physically, some emotionally, but most of all, he would touch the hearts of the people coming up front for prayer. I was able to see God love on people as he brought fresh hope to the ones feeling hopeless.

I found out quickly that I would encounter divine appointments outside the church walls, in restaurants, gas stations, and other places. All I knew was that I loved watching God change lives.

The Youth Pastor at the time, John Hoffman, asked me to work with the junior high boys and girls on Friday nights at F.C.F. I served in that ministry for about one and a half years. The most powerful move I had experienced in the power of the Holy Spirit was when I was a counselor at junior high camp at F.C.F. for the summer. I had prayed, asking God to give me the toughest group of boys for my cabin. I soon found out, that you need to be careful what you ask for because sometimes it is what you receive, and I received just that.

God showed up in a big way, and three out of eight boys got saved the first night. The rest of the five boys were already saved but ended up in an unruly group.

We were all at camp worship the next night, and one of the women counselors had a severe headache, so she asked me for an aspirin. So we went to my truck, and I was in such a hurry to get back inside to hear the message, I dropped all of the aspirin on the ground. I then said, let me pray for you instead of taking medicine. Not only did the Lord heal her headache, but His Spirit fell on the whole camp. 12- and 13-year-old junior high kids were receiving prayer language and receiving the Spirit of joy and laughter too. God was healing broken and wounded hearts from abandonment, abuse of parents, along with the wounds from parents getting divorced.

The very next week was high school camp, and God showed up, but it wasn't the same magnitude. I think it is because junior high school boys and girls are more open, less corrupt and a lot more innocent than the high school boys and girls. Therefore, God seemed to be able to enter their hearts easier.

I shared all that to say this: I will never forget the day that some of us from the singles ministry from Foothills Christian Fellowship rode the bus to chaperone the junior high and high school kids for a Greg Laurie "HARVEST CRUSADE" held at the San Diego Jack Murphy Stadium.

Here is how sneaky Satan is. He cannot read our minds and can only use and tempt us with our history as he tries to bring Shame and Guilt into our lives. (See Shame Chapter 2; and Guilt Chapter 3.)

As I said earlier, I came to faith in Christ at the San Diego Jack Murphy Stadium at 16 years of age. Now I was in the same stadium for a Christian event. The crusade was incredible and a huge success. I chaperoned some of the junior and senior high school kids and watched them give their lives to Jesus, as I had done on the same field 23 years earlier.

Allow me to back up for a minute. As we entered the stadium, a young woman was running to catch up with her group. She tried to skirt the crowd by sliding against the chain-link fence. In doing so, her tennis shoe caught on the bottom of the fence, and she tripped and fell. She fell to the pavement with excruciating pain in her left ankle.

I walked up to her to politely ask if I could pray for her, and she responded with a hesitant yes! I don't know what she expected, but I fully expected God to heal her ankle so she could join her friends and enjoy the event.

I prayed a simple prayer, taking authority in Jesus' name over the pain and swelling, which was rather large already. The Holy Spirit rocked her world as the swelling and pain left her ankle. A couple of us helped her to her feet as she stated that the pain had gone entirely; she started to walk on it with absolutely no limping. She then briskly walked away from us towards the stadium entry gate and headed into the stadium.

Immediately following the "Harvest Crusade," we headed for the bus, where we would wait for everyone. There were 14 or 15 of us in a circle sharing about the Crusade, so I asked if anyone had a need for physical healing or just wanted a fresh infilling of the Holy Spirit. One of my male friends, Jim, wanted prayer for damage done to his shoulder from a softball game injury the previous week, along with several other males and females with knee pain.

I asked my friends, Chuck and Mark, who were tall, muscular guys, to stand behind each person I was going to pray for as we stood on the asphalt. Not all, but sometimes, when the Holy Spirit comes upon a person, he or she may find it difficult to remain standing. Some call this being "slain in the Spirit." I prefer to call it, "resting in the Spirit." God often does deep works in people's lives during these times.

I laid hands on Jim's shoulder, and God profoundly touched him. He began to shake and told me his shoulder felt like it was on fire. I explained to him that sometimes that happens when God is healing someone, and as I finished that statement, Chuck and Mark laid Jim gently on the asphalt. Yes, Jim was "resting in the Spirit."

I continued praying for those with knee pain and all of those people also ended up on the asphalt. Mark, one the men catching those falling from God's presence on them, asked for prayer for his neck injury from a car accident five years previously.

Chuck walked over and stood behind Mark as I laid hands on his neck and prayed. I took authority over the trauma from the car accident as well as the damage done to his body. Even though Mark was taller than Chuck, the Holy Spirit helped Chuck lay Mark gently down on the asphalt.

Several of the stadium security men saw what was happening and came running over thinking there was a fight with people lying on the asphalt. I explained to them that everyone was ok and that all of those lying on the pavement was safe and that it was a move of God. They looked at me like I had two heads and just walked away.

How does a Ministry Blind Spot get birthed?

As the security men walked away, I turned around and looked at everyone lying on the asphalt still in the presence of God. Suddenly, this thought came into my mind; "Look what I just did!" I had taken credit for the work of the Holy Spirit. No one but God, Satan and I knew that I had taken credit for the healing presence of God!

Satan's scheme:

Satan already knew three things about me that day!

- I came to faith in that stadium 23-years earlier.
- I walked away from God for seventeen and one-half years.
- I had just taken credit for God's working hand through the Holy Spirit at that same stadium.

Satan was trying to fill me with such shame and guilt that I wouldn't pray for people anymore, and maybe quit going to church altogether.

Years before I was ordained as a Vineyard pastor in 2007, Satan tried to create a Ministry Blind Spot in my life. He knew that as a young man and into adulthood, I had a problem with pride and rebellion. So, it seemed good to him to distract me by bringing pride back into my life again. (See Pride & Rebellion Chapter 9.)

After everyone got up off the asphalt, and all that came with us had returned to the bus, we headed back to the church. I was reticent as God was already dealing with my prideful heart

On the trip back on the bus, I heard my friends exchanging testimonies of what happened in the stadium as well as those I had laid hands on in the parking lot. I remained quiet and acted as if I was tired and just wanted to rest. When we arrived at the church, we all got off the bus and went our separate ways.

After I rededicated my life to Jesus in 1995, I spent a significant amount of time in God's word and memorized Scripture.

As I drove home, Scriptures began to flood my mind like a gentle waterfall in the forest. The Lord reminded me of the verse having to do with pride coming before a fall.

> *Pride goes before destruction, a haughty spirit before a fall* (Proverbs 16:18).

The same Holy Spirit who had earlier healed my friends in the stadium parking lot was now convicting me for taking credit for what God had done. I pulled my car to the side of the road and tearfully asked God to forgive me. He did. He graciously prevented me from continuing to minister with that Blind Spot!

I thanked Him for revealing my haughty heart as yet another Scripture passage came to mind.

> *Create in me a pure heart, O God, and renew a steadfast spirit within me. Do not cast me from your presence or take your Holy Spirit from me* (Psalm 51:10-11).

John Wimber, the founder of the Vineyard Movement, would say that it would be one or more of "the three G's" that would cause men of God to fall from ministry. They were *glory*, *gold*, and *girls*.

How might these three Ministry Blind Spots look?

As I've said, as I ministered at the stadium, Satan tempted me to take credit for God's glory.

What about when men or women who get into a ministry, especially a healing ministry, and have no pastoral covering and aren't accountable to anyone? As a pastor, I call those people loose cannons or rogue ministers!

Their followers tend to be people who are also not plugged into a local church. They convince themselves that the ministry they follow is the only one that can heal people. Sometimes these so-called healers begin to listen to their followers and start believing they are uniquely chosen to carry a special anointing for God!

Sometimes, those who follow these leaders are like "groupies" following a rock band from concert to concert, chasing the Holy Spirit.

They continually pump up those in healing ministries to where it becomes all about them! In other words, pride begins to set in for the heads of these ministries as well as the followers too. They start to see the healing and miracles as if they had some credit in them happening, just as I did when I made that dreadful decision to take credit for God's glory at the Jack Murphy stadium that night.

The second of the three Blind Spots is gold. I've also heard of other pastors having to step down from the ministry due to a Ministry Blind Spot related to the gold. Their ministry focus turned to money.

I've had Pastor friends who fell due to a Ministry Blind related to girls. Satan tempted them with females who appeared to be interested in their ministry. One thing led to another, and soon their marriages and ministries were destroyed by adulterous affairs.

Over 20 years ago, two of my good friends were asked to step down from ministry. One was a young pastor that I felt was too immature to ordain at the time. The other one was a lay leader who had adopted an unbiblical philosophy. The young pastor became fascinated by the lay leader's heresy, which led to a Ministry Blind Spot that gave way to pride and rebellion. Soon, neither of them were willing to receive correction from the senior leaders.

As a pastor through the years, fortunately, I have asked less than a handful of people to step down due to a Ministry Blind Spot. One of them was a prideful man, which was on the prayer team that acted like a good Christian man within the church walls but treated his wife with disrespect outside the church building. Another one was a man on a worship team that I found out was leading a blatant sinful life at home, and when confronted, he denied it.

The last people I had asked to step down from ministry, was a married couple who were two of my leaders. They couldn't admit that their bad attitudes were emotionally disturbing some of my flock and refused to submit to my pastoral authority.

Sometimes a pastor can be very lonely. How can that be, you might ask? Pastors are around many people throughout the week. True. However, the attention is focused on the parishioners as we minister to them. Pastors can find it hard to develop close friendships, which can lead to loneliness, especially for my introvert pastor friends. Other than my wife, family, and friends, I spend a lot of quiet time with Abba, and in God's Word.

Pastors need close Christian relationships to share real life with, as it is very critical for the longevity of their ministry. Pastors need other leaders to minister to them on a regular basis.

Another Ministry Blind Spot in churches that is hardly ever recognized before it is too late is burnout. Pastors on staff, other paid leaders on the team, and lay leaders can be burned out and not even realize it.

Burnout can cause significant physical fatigue, stress that can lead to anger, irritability, being short with people, along with being very combative towards others at church and at home too. Burnout can also cause a pastor or leader to isolate, which can lead to depression, other various behaviors that might also lead to a "closet-sin" lifestyle. The absolute saddest thing about ministry burnout is when it brings forth self-judgment that leads to condemnation, carrying on a depressive state that leads to isolation, which has led to some suicides.

In smaller churches, pastors, and their wives usually handle 80 percent of the workload and lay workers pick up the remaining 20 percent. Many small church pastors are bi-vocational. The many hours spent between the marketplace job and church work can lead to burnout. In small church settings, it would typically be the pastor's spouse that would see and point out the Ministry Blind Spot of burnout.

What makes a larger church pastor successful? Some would say if he or she has a large flock. Others would say if they're holding more than one service on Sundays and still others would say if there were a large tithe base.

Senior pastors should have great leadership teams around them to oversee all the ministries, allowing them the freedom they need to do what God has called them to do to fulfill the church's vision.

The leadership team needs to be in unity to be able to see burnout in the pastor(s) as well others on the leadership team. Real integration with pastors and their leadership team, allows each one of the team to speak truth to each other with constructive criticism. This type of authentic unity can prevent ministry burnout.

A pastor with God's vision and a great leadership team tends to cultivate a community that is attractive to newcomers/guests. This type of community loves, encourages, and is very supportive to help new converts, and Christians that have moved to the local community to find their way towards God's vision for their life.

Once a new person has come to the church, has bought into the pastor's vision, gets plugged into a small group, joins a men's or women's growth group, they are on their way to becoming a disciple of Jesus. Within six months to a year, they should be in or heading towards God's specific calling on their life.

The primary key to prevent Ministry Blind Spot burnout is Sabbath rest. Everyone in ministry needs to take time off, get away from the weekly fast pace, day-in-day-out, the hustle, and bustle of the church business.

If you are in full-time, part-time or marketplace ministry, take a vacation, spend time with family, have fun and enjoy time off.

When a pastor(s) have a great leadership team, it gives the confidence to take the vacation for Sabbath rest.

On top of all that, every pastor needs to have a mentor. This mentor can be younger or older; age has no bearing on mentoring as long as he or she is more mature in Christ.

NOTE: Pastors should never pick a mentor that is afraid to speak truth into his or her life. The fact a pastor needs to hear from his or her mentor is when the pastor is out-of-sorts! The cause could be from ministry distraction that leads to a Ministry Blind Spot, which is evident to those who are in direct relationship with the pastor.

Questions to ponder and room to write as you leave this chapter!

How was this chapter helpful in my current circumstances?

_____
_____
_____
_____

How is the Ministry I'm involved in all about me?

_____
_____
_____
_____

What problems am I ignoring in Ministry?

_____
_____

How am I married to Ministry?

How am I hurting people through Ministry

What are my next steps to move towards freedom in Ministry?

Remember,

God desires to heal you emotionally, physically and spiritually!

Before entering the next chapter on Deception, please pause and pray this prayer:

Father God, thank you for highlighting and revealing my Ministry Blind Spot.

As I learn not to be in a Ministry Blind Spot, I release all of the stuff on my mind right now. I give it to you God, and I receive your peace.

Thank you, Holy Spirit, for replacing the Ministry Blind Spot thoughts with your words of truth.

Father God, I realize just reading this book is not enough for total healing, so I pray that you will place the right pastors, leaders, counselors, and friends who understand me to walk the rest of this healing journey with me.

I pray these things in Jesus name! Amen.

Your new friend,

Pastor Mark

Chapter 16
Deception

All deception in the course of life is indeed nothing else but a lie reduced to practice, and falsehood passing from words into things. -- **Robert Southey**

What is deception?

Deception is the action of deceiving someone.

Manipulation can never cultivate a real relationship or a healthy community.

Healthy communities can only come from cultivating honesty and truth.

There is a reason to get good references before having a contractor build your home. Why?

Otherwise, you end up with a home that won't make it through the storms.

When asking people what the first step is when building a home, most people will say, "build a strong foundation!" There absolutely must be a strong foundation. However, a strong foundation will only work built on stable soil. The soil must be prepared and compacted as well as pass a soil compaction test to pull a permit to build.

What does the Bible say about building a house on good soil?

Everyone then who hears these words of mine and does them will be like a wise man who built his house on the rock. 25 And the rain fell, and the floods came, and the winds blew and beat on that house, but it did

> *not fall, because it had been founded on the rock. 26 And everyone who hears these words of mine and does not do them will be like a foolish man who built his house on the sand. 27 And the rain fell, and the floods came, and the winds blew and beat against that house, and it fell, and great was the fall of it* (Matthew 7:24-27, ESV).

The scary and most devastating part of deception is when someone is being deceived and doesn't have a clue.

This Blind Spot can destroy relationships through manipulation.

What about a person that is in a Deception Blind Spot to themselves and doesn't realize it? You might be thinking; how this can happen.

It's no different than a beautiful rose garden that has weeds below the surface. In other words, everything appears to look right above the ground. The roses are beautiful, healthy, and colorfully vibrant, as they all flourish with incredible fragrance, and all visible surface weeds have been attended to and dealt with and put into the recycle bin.

It's not the pulled weeds that are the problem they are gone!

What do we know about weeds?

Weeds are sneaky, like Satan coming in through a Blind Spot.

Weeds rob the proper nutrients from the soil.

Weeds steal water that the roses in this story need to survive.

Weeds are liars as they pretend to look like non-offensive blades of grass or are disguised flowers.

Let's face it. When we buy sod, grass seed or even fruit trees, they inevitably come with unwanted weeds. There is never a need to plant weeds because they are always there. However, with Blind Spots, we are constantly planting weeds in relationships.

Weeds That Persuade

What weeds keep us from a relationship with Father God?

What weeds are in the way when we are reading and studying God's Word?

What weeds are in the way to keeps us from going to church or weekly Bible studies?

What are the weeds in your heart that need removal?

God desires that all people repent and be saved.

> *The Lord is not slow about His promise, as some count slowness, but is patient toward you, not wishing for any to perish but for all to come to repentance* (2 Peter 3:9, NASB).

At the same time, Satan, the "father of lies deceives the very people who need to accept the truth."

> *You are of your father the devil, and you want to do the desires of your father. He was a murderer from the beginning and does not stand in the truth because there is no truth in him. Whenever he speaks a lie, he speaks from his own nature, for he is a liar and the father of lies* (John 8:44, NASB).

> *Just look at your own calling, believers; not many [of you were considered] wise according to human standards, not many powerful or influential, not many of high and noble birth* (1 Corinthians 1:26, AMP).

The god of this age has blinded the minds of unbelievers, so they cannot see the light of the gospel of the glory of Christ.

> *in whose case the god of this world has blinded the minds of the unbelieving so that they might not see the light of the gospel of the glory of Christ, who is the image of God* (2 Corinthians 4:4, NASB).

The Bible presents a consistent snapshot of how sin and deception are related.

The way we tend to think of deceit is a bit deceived. If we are talking spiritual, deception is more profound than merely being tricked or lied too. For us getting saved, we don't require any level of intelligence, philosophical ability, or wisdom.

> *But seek first his kingdom and his righteousness, and all these things will be given to you as well* (Matthew 6:33).

Matthew 6:33 is one of my favorite Scripture passages. To thoroughly understand it, one must know what "the kingdom of God" refers to. The kingdom of God is anywhere He rules and reigns. It's where His presence and power are evident. Examples would include our exercising the authority given to us by Jesus to cast out demons, heal the sick, bring sight to the blind, and to free the captives.

If we understand the kingdom as the rule and reign of Jesus on Earth, then we can stand in His righteousness, and things added. What are these added things?

We must backtrack to see it.

Explained in Matthew 6:31-32, *So do not worry, saying, 'What shall we eat?' or 'What shall we drink? 'or 'What shall we wear?'*

32 For the pagans run after all these things, and your heavenly Father knows that you need them.

When we focus on His kingdom and His righteousness, we won't be distracted by Satan, and begin to worry about our provisions like food, clothing, or drink. We focus intimately on Jehovah Jireh (our great Provider), knowing that He will provide for our every need. Then we can teach others to do likewise.

In Matthew 13:19, *When anyone hears the message about the kingdom and does not understand it, the evil one comes and snatches away what was sown in their heart. This is the seed sown along the path.*

Jesus has sown the seed of His authority and power in every believer.

If we as followers of Jesus don't understand Matthew 13:19, and what the kingdom is, we can lead a defeated life as the devil makes us think that he has more power than we do. This defeat comes right out of the pit of hell!

When we come to Christ, we have the same power that raised Jesus from the dead!

We need to walk in that power because we have all received the same authority that Jesus gave his disciples as He ascended into the clouds!

Unfortunately, as humans, we have a habit of using increased knowledge to develop more sophisticated ways to sin.

Weeds are only one problem! The bigger one is when we have planted in the wrong soil!

How often do we genuinely take the time to check and see if we have proper soil before planting?

We must make sure that there are no slabs of concrete, boulders, various rocks or any other obstructions to keep roots from going deep to get the water needed for the plant above the ground.

In the story of the parable of the sower, Jesus lays out the various soils,

> *Listen then to what the parable of the sower means: 19 When anyone hears the message about the kingdom and does not understand it, the evil one comes and snatches away what was sown in their heart. This is the seed sown along the path. 20 The seed falling on rocky ground refers to someone who hears the word and at once receives it with joy. 21 But since they have no root, they last only a short time. When trouble or persecution comes because of the word, they quickly fall away. 22 The seed falling among the thorns refers to someone who hears the word, but the worries of this life and the deceitfulness of wealth choke the word, making it unfruitful. 23 But the seed falling on good soil refers to someone who hears the word and understands it. This is the one who produces a crop, yielding a hundred, sixty or thirty times what was sown* (Matthew 13:18-23).

We can't sow seeds of His truth and His power if we don't understand His kingdom principles!

Let's also remember that we are all one body of Christ, and God shows no favoritism.

> *There is neither Jew nor Greek, there is neither slave nor free, there is neither male nor female; for you are all one in Christ Jesus* (Galatians 3:28, NKJV).

What seeds are you sowing?

> *Do not be deceived: God is not mocked, for whatever one sows, that will he also reap* (Galatians 6:7).

Satan tried sowing a seed of deception to God and ended up deceived by his Blind Spot. (See "Where Did Blind Spots Originate?" in Chapter 1.)

Just as we can't see the weeds below the surface of the ground in our garden, so it was that Satan didn't see the hidden consequence of an irreversible decision he made, wanting to be like God.

The last thing on a person's mind, who is committing a known sin, is the potentially devastating consequences that their search for immediate gratification may bring. Some of these adverse consequences might only last a day, a week or year, and yet other times, it can be a lifetime of a devastating circumstance(s).

For instance, a dear brother in Christ and pastor of over 20 years before becoming a Christian had made a super bad decision that affects him every day of his life.

Before he got saved, he had a severe street drug past. In a season of Meth, he was awake for over a week straight. Even though he was super tired, he still made the wrong decision to drive his car a long distance. As he drove, he fell asleep at the wheel, veered off the road, and hit a stabilizing cable on a rather large, sturdy power pole. His car flipped, and he broke his neck, causing severe spinal injuries that put him in a wheelchair for the rest of his life.

Before my friend in the above story gave his life to Jesus, he was on the broad road of destruction!

> *When tempted, no one should say, "God is tempting me." For God cannot be tempted by evil, nor does he tempt anyone; 14 but each person is tempted when they are dragged away by their own evil desire and enticed. 15 Then, after desire has conceived, it gives birth to sin; and sin, when it is full-grown, gives birth to death. 16 Don't be deceived, my dear brothers and sisters. 17 Every good and perfect gift is from above, coming down from the Father of the heavenly lights,*

who does not change like shifting shadows. 18 He chose to give us birth through the word of truth, that we might be a kind of firstfruits of all he created (James 1:14-27).

Enter through the narrow gate. For wide is the gate and broad is the road that leads to destruction, and many enter through it. 14 But small is the gate and narrow the road that leads to life, and only a few find it (Matthew 7:13-14).

Questions to ponder and room to write as you leave this chapter!

How was this chapter helpful in my current circumstances?

_____
_____
_____
_____

How am I ignoring a Deception problem in my life?

_____
_____
_____
_____

How has my Deception hurt others?

_____
_____
_____
_____

What are my next steps to move towards freedom in Deception?

_____
_____
_____
_____

God already knows what you need before you even ask Him!

Before entering the next chapter on Unforgiveness, please pause and pray this prayer:

Father God, thank you for highlighting and revealing my Blind Spot of Deception. I choose to exchange Deception for honesty.

> *If we claim to have fellowship with him and yet walk in the darkness, we lie and do not live out the truth*
> (1 John 1:6)

As I continue to walk out my journey in healing with you, please help me to stay in Your word as you open the door to take the proper steps in dissolving the damage done to my relationships. Thank you, Holy Spirit, for replacing those thoughts of Deception with your words of truth.

Father God, I realize just reading this book is not enough for total healing, so I pray that you will place the right pastors, leaders, counselors, and friends who understand me to walk the rest of this healing journey with me.

I pray these things in Jesus' name! Amen.

Your new friend,

Pastor Mark

Chapter 17

Unforgiveness

For one to hold Unforgiveness toward another will become crippling. It will cause unwanted stress on us, and our relationships with God, and others.

Young children generally don't hold grudges. They may cry and throw tantrums, but when done, they seem to be able to let it go. Adults, however, tend to hang on to offenses that lead to unforgiveness.

When people do wrong to our loved ones or us, our human nature wants them to pay for what they've done, and to suffer as we have. To the natural mind, it only seems fair to expect restitution of some kind. Unless this occurs, we tend to withhold forgiveness, which in turn ultimately hurts us emotionally, physically, and spiritually, and not the offender.

As Christians, we are all called to a different standard and way of thinking, one that's consistent with God's character. God is a merciful Father who wants His children to show mercy to others.

For instance, when someone cuts us off in traffic, whether intentional or unintentional, either way, God wants us not to bite the bait, run with the offense, or harbor bitterness that leads to unforgiveness. (Blind Spot of Offense see Chapter 6)

Be merciful, just as your Father is merciful
(Luke 6:36).

Jesus' life on Earth demonstrated this as he hung on the cross. He prayed for those who crucified Him.

> *Jesus said, "Father, forgive them, for they do not know what they are doing." And they divided up his clothes by casting lots* (Luke 23:34).

God expects us to forgive as Jesus did, regardless of the circumstances.

This command seems impossible to carry out until we start to grasp the enormity of what took place on the cross. Christ's death gives fresh daily mercy that is so great that it defies comprehension. Jesus, as our Savior, took all our sin upon Him and died in our place. He experienced the outpouring of God's wrath that leads us to reconciliation with the Father. Although we deserve condemnation, through Jesus Christ, we have instead received God's unmerited favor, which is mercy.

Now, as new creations in Christ who are indwelt by the Holy Spirit, we have His power to honestly let go of the wrongs done to us and extend mercy to others, just as God has and continues daily to extend His mercy to us.

Let's stop here for second and ponder on this! Do you realize that God will not forgive you unless you forgive others first?

> *For if you forgive other people when they sin against you, your heavenly Father will also forgive you. But if you do not forgive others their sins, your Father will not forgive your sins* (Matthew 6:14-15).

Maybe a family member died, and now you're mad at God. In the book of Job in the Bible, we see where God takes family members from Job.

> The LORD gave and the LORD has taken away; may the name of the LORD be praised." In all this, Job did not sin by charging God with wrongdoing (Job 1:21b-22).

Or perhaps you just lost a job that you prayed so hard to get, or you didn't get the girlfriend or boyfriend you wanted, and you just gave up on that prayer.

Have you ever thought that God was trying to redirect your prayers, as He already knows what we need and that what we want can lead us in a wrong direction for the plans he has for us?

> For I know the plans that I have for you,' declares the LORD, 'plans for welfare and not for calamity to give you a future and a hope (Jeremiah 29:11, NASB).

Satan's job becomes easy, and he loves it when we blame God and refuse to forgive Him!

Ponder this. Before you lost that job, did you pray in submission by seeking God's face for the best position for you, or did you pray, "God, I want that job."

God created human beings, not robots, and we all have our own will.

God Loves us enough to give us exactly what we want in an expectation that what we want will bring us to Him. What do I mean by this?

When God throws a life raft out to us in a storm of life, instead of us climbing into the life raft, we pull so hard on the life raft that the rope God is holding onto eventually slips through His fingers.

We must forgive God, to move to our next step, which is to forgive others.

Here's another area of unforgiveness that Satan will use to hold you captive. If you don't, can't, or won't forgive yourself for sinning against yourself or others!

When we finally submit to God and embrace His love that hung on the cross, we can then forgive God and others too. There are other times though, where there still seems to be a legitimate unease that continues to hang on!

You begin to question yourself, what is it? I've forgiven God and all those I needed to, so what is this unease that I'm still feeling? I know God created me to be at rest, but I'm not.

As you ponder this question, you must remember that feelings are not right or wrong, they are what they are!

Often, we will forgive God and others too, but we forget to forgive someone that is super special and is close to us. That particular person is YOU!

How do you know when you have unequivocally without a doubt forgiven someone? Answer at the end of this chapter.

The definition of unforgiveness speaks for itself: being unwilling or unable to forgive.

Adolf Coors the III had been kidnapped and brutally murdered. Adolf Coors the IV was the grandson of Coors Brewery founder in 1873, and he says it like this:

(Paraphrased) Unforgiveness is like pouring acid on someone else's heart, but because it comes from your heart first, the acid is already destroying your own heart!

In November 1995, I owned Executive Construction company. I received a phone call one morning from a Mr. and Mrs. Russell, who wanted a home remodel. That afternoon, I headed to Chula Vista, California from my office in El Cajon, to provide estimates for enclosing a patio, a bathroom and kitchen remodel, which would bring in a substantial sum of money.

I arrived at my prospective clients' home around 11:45 AM and was invited to sit with them at their dining room table to discuss their project. Mrs. Russell excused herself and went into the kitchen to make us some sandwiches and iced tea for lunch.

Mr. and Mrs. Russell were Christians, so we hit it off right away.

While she was in the kitchen, her husband told me a story of how his wife had not heard from her father for 25 years. We also talked about the Lord and physical healing, as his wife's left knee had been in pain for many years. I asked him if she would be willing for me to pray for her knee to get healed. About that same time, she came out with our lunch on a platter in one hand and a pitcher of fresh brewed iced tea in the other. We all ate lunch together, talked about Jesus, and discussed where we currently attended church.

I was more concerned about Mrs. Russell's need for healing than I was about signing a construction contract.

Immediately following lunch, all three of us went into the living room so I could anoint her knee with oil and pray for healing. I anointed her knee and invited the kingdom to come as I took authority in Jesus' name over the pain and commanded healing.

The Holy Spirit rocked her as she began to shake and weep. As I felt the Lord speak to me about unforgiveness in her heart towards her estranged father. I asked Mrs. Russell if there was a relationship in her life that was in disarray. She told me that due to deep emotional hurt she hadn't spoken to her dad in more than 25 years.

I asked Mrs. Russell if she would permit God to change her heart to forgive her dad for the things he had done to her.

As she gave God permission, the forgiveness she couldn't previously offer and didn't want to, came flowing from her lips, and as it did, her knee made a loud popping sound.

God had revealed a Blind Spot of Unforgiveness in Mrs. Russell life. She said "I'm free," as she shouted out with joy, and began jumping up and down on both legs, screaming out that her knee no longer hurt her.

We all got to witness God move in such a miraculous physical healing and emotional heart restoration through forgiveness for her dad.

Two hours after arriving at the house, I wrote the work orders for the three remodels, and Mr. and Mrs. Russell signed them.

It was three weeks to the day when my company began the projects at their home.

Two weeks into the job, as I sat on the back deck my company had just completed, I was eating lunch when Mr. and Mrs. Russell came running out onto the porch all excited.

God had already moved so powerfully in both of their lives the day of the signed contract.

Now, check this out! After Mrs. Russell got healed, she and her husband had not told anyone, especially her dad that lived back east.

However, God did something powerful in the Spirit realm, because Mrs. Russell was standing in front of me with tears running down her cheeks, with a birthday card from her estranged dad of 25 years, that she just received five minutes earlier in the mail. She handed me the card to read, that was asking her to please find it in her heart to forgive him for all the hurt that he caused in her life.

By the time my company finished all the remodeling, Mrs. Russell and her dad had spoken on the phone several times. As they continued their restored relationship, she and her husband were planning a trip back east to visit her dad after the remodel.

I didn't learn forgiveness as a young man. I learned to hold grudges. My dad grew up with a dad and grandfather that were egotistical and brutal over disciplinarians. My dad ran away from home at 13 years old and jumped a cargo train with a friend to head to Montana from Washington State. My dad and his friend worked for a sheep ranch in Montana. When my dad turned 15 and one-half and weighed 180 pounds, he changed his name and joined the army.

While in the army, my dad met my mom and wanted to marry her. He checked into getting his name changed back and found out that his given name by my grandmother wasn't his name recorded on his birth certificate. Due to the wrong name recorded on my dad's birth certificate, the government told my dad to keep his title as Don Baxter.

Here are two significant reasons my dad learned to hold a grudge rather than to forgive. Depending on your upbringing, these reasons might resonate with you as well, or spark something in your own unforgiving heart.

- When my dad was born in a lumber milling camp in Washington State, my dad's mom had my great grandfather register his birth. Instead of entering my dad's name as his given name by my grandmother, my dads mom, before his birth, as Richard Burke, my great-grandfather wrote down my dad as his first name-middle name, Burke the III, and never told anyone.

- My grandfather, instead of using a belt or paddle on my dad, used two brutal forms of discipline; one type was a razor strap that was used to sharpen shaving razors, and the other one was an ironing cord which in those days removed from the iron. Not only was my grandfather brutal to my dad, but also while my dad was in the army, he sent money home for my grandparents (his mom and dad) to save for him until he could come back on military leave, only to find that they spent it all.

Through the abuse my dad endured from his parents as a young man on into adulthood, without realizing it, he picked up a Blind Spot of Unforgiveness.

Unforgiveness has been scientifically proven outside of God's word to cause stress, which can lead to anxiety. (See Anxiety & Worry in Chapter 5.)

The Bible explains it as Dis-Ease. According to the Bible, we were created to be at rest. When we have anything other than peace and rest, we need to find out why. When an officer in the military addresses a platoon, they immediately come to attention due to the authority standing before them.

After military inspection, the words "at-ease" are said. The at-ease/rest is 24/7 with Jesus as our commanding/servant/officer.

To get a picture of this, please pause here read these three short passages.

Matthew 11:28-30

Ephesians 4:31

Luke 23:33-34

Very few people could read in the first century. They would meet together where the Old Testament was read to them. Matthew 11:28-30 (above) depicts a lamb running as fast as possible, while its ribs are ripped to the bone and bleeding from the claws of the wolf or bear pursuing it.

> During World War II, Austrian neurologist Victor Frankl lived in concentration camps. During the years Victor lived there, through his relationship with God, he spent many hours leading people through repentance and forgiveness before walking into and dying in gas chambers.

God used a South African man, Desmond TuTu, to bring total forgiveness to South Africa through his famous quote, "No future without forgiveness."

So, let me ask this, if a person refuses to forgive someone that has hurt them, then why does that person want to rent or lease out space in their mind to continually think about that person(s)?

What do I mean by this and where am I going with this statement?

Pause and ponder this question: What offense(s) are you still holding on to that is causing your Unforgiveness?

I want you to leave this last chapter of this book with this statement: Forgiving a person is not you saying that the offense done to you was OK!

What forgiving does, is like Leah Coulter—my former Masters professor—says in her book, *Repentance & Forgiveness*; "Put the offense in the Court Room of God's Heart."

In other words, when we refuse to forgive, this is the picture! It is as if we are in a prison cell and the person we refuse to forgive holds the key to that prison cell. When we forgive, the key to that prison cell will appear.

Depending on the offense done to us and the emotional hurt caused by that offense, the process length can equal that offense. What do I mean by this? Just as pain tolerance depends on the person with that pain, so it is with the understanding of an offense.

When we choose not to forgive, it only continues to hurt us and not the offender.

As a pastor, I ask the person holding onto that offense if they are willing to permit God to change their heart to want to forgive the person that hurt them.

Who are you carrying around to weigh you down?

There are several Internet posts on stress, etc. causing physical harm to physical organs.

With headlines warning us of international terrorism, global warming, and economic uncertainty, we're all likely to be a little more anxious these days.

As an everyday emotion, anxiety the "fight or flight" response can be a good thing, prompting us to take extra precautions. But when anxiety persists in the absence of a need to fight or flee, it can not only interfere with our daily lives but also undermine our physical health.

Here is just one Internet post on effects of stress:

> Evidence suggests that people with anxiety disorders are at greater risk for developing a number of chronic medical conditions. They may also have more severe symptoms and a greater risk of death when they become ill. Harvard Women's Health Watch— Updated: June 6, 2017 first published: July 2008.

As you leave this last chapter in your journey in this book, I told you that I would answer the opening question to this chapter: how do you know when you have, unequivocally, without a doubt forgiven someone?

Here is your answer: The way you know if total forgiveness has happened is by examining the feelings that come up in your heart. Is it hate, anger, anxiety, or is the feeling of hurt and emotional pain finally gone when the person you supposedly have forgiven, is seen at a distance, is in your immediate presence, or their name is brought up in conversation?

God will heal our broken hearts from relationships gone bad, and the pain will gradually subside. He allows the memory to remain so we can help others process their pain.

Questions to ponder and room to write as you leave the last chapter of this book!

How was this chapter helpful in my current circumstances?

_____
_____
_____
_____

What Unforgiveness do I still carry?

_____
_____
_____
_____

How has Unforgiveness affected my health or caused stress etc.?

_____
_____
_____
_____

What are my next steps to move towards freedom from Unforgiveness?

_____
_____
_____
_____

Father God, thank you for highlighting and revealing my Blind Spot of Unforgiveness. I repent. Forgive me.

As I finish the last chapter of this book, I choose to exchange Unforgiveness for your peace that surpasses all understanding.

> *And the peace of God, which transcends all understanding, will guard your hearts and your minds in Christ Jesus* (Philippians 4:7).

As I continue to walk out my journey in healing with you, please help me to read your Word as you open the door to take steps in dissolving the damage done to my relationships.

All of the stuff on my mind right now, I give it to you God, and I receive your peace where Unforgiveness resided in my heart.

Thank you, Holy Spirit, for replacing those thoughts of Unforgiveness with your words of truth. You know what concerns me; I choose to guard my heart, not to allow Unforgiveness to control my life, and to now focus my mind on what truth is in the midst turmoil I may face because I know you go before me and you have my back.

Father God, I realize just reading this book is not enough for total healing, so I pray that you will place the right pastors, leaders, counselors, and friends who understand me to walk the rest of this healing journey with me.

I pray these things in Jesus' name! Amen.

I pray as you seek God in this, that he will not only heal your past, but he will help you in your present, heading into the future. Remember, God is always pursuing and deepening his relationship with you.

Your new friend,

Pastor Mark

EPILOGUE

We all have busy lives, so I want to thank you for taking the time to read my book.

Whether you took the time to read every chapter or found the chapter(s) in the table of contents that applied to your life journey and read only those; I hope you found some resolve, along with new ideas for dealing with any past, present and future Blind Spots in your life.

Hopefully, as you took the journey through my book, you now have in mind a Blind Spot(s) that a co-worker, a friend or a family member may have that you can share your testimony with of how this book helped you. Also, as you have dealt with one or more of your Blind Spots, you will now find some avenues to point out, respectfully, a Blind Spot(s) that you see in their lives.

If you don't want to give someone your book to read, thank you for directing him or her to where they can purchase his or her copy.

After I wrote this book and reread it several times before publishing it, I was reminded that no book one will write is enough for anyone's total healing. So, I pray that God will put the right friends, pastors, leaders, and counselors to walk the rest of this healing journey with you.

If you are a follower of Christ, I pray as you seek God in this, that he will not only heal your past, but he will help you in your present relationships as you head into the future.

Remember, God is daily pursuing you for a deeper relationship with Him and one day,

The wolf will live with the lamb, the leopard will lie down with the goat, the calf and the lion and the yearling together (Isaiah 11:6b).

Until then, God can help us to restore broken relationships and to develop new, unlikely friendships as we continue to see our Blind Spot(s).

May, we with His sweet undeniable and loving grace, walk in repenting hearts and restore damaged and broken past and present relationships!

May, we with His same grace, point out in Love, the Blind Spot(s) of our friends and walk the journey with them to restore their damaged and broken relationships too.

Dear Father God, as followers of Christ Jesus, help us to break down barriers and seek to befriend others. As we do, enable us to be bearers of the gospel of peace.

I hope you will sleep in peace tonight. I pray these things in Jesus name, Amen.

Your new friend,

Pastor Mark

Appendix
Process of Identity

Before we are born in the flesh, we are in a sort of darkness, not knowing our identity yet! The day we leave the womb, we begin a journey of learning and growing in our identity.

- First: Even though we couldn't quite understand it, everything we needed to survive was inside the womb, and now after leaving the womb, we immediately begin to recognize that the same person that did that for us is now holding us and embracing us as we, in turn, embrace them!

- Second: We begin to realize that we are being fed and cared for each time we desire and need it.

- Third: Each day we realize we wake up to a repeated pattern of what we later learn is love!

It is the same pattern: when we are born again/our new and designed identity through the Trinitarian Godhead!

12 Stages To Discovering Our True Identity In Christ

1. The Holy Spirit draws us towards Father God out of our lost state.

2. We give our lives to Jesus by confessing our need of a Savior.
3. We begin to walk out our sonship or daughtership in Christ Jesus.
4. We join a local Bible-believing church if we aren't already.
5. The Holy Spirit, who lives in us, gradually transforms us from the inside out.
6. We realize that it's no longer about us. Our focus turns to Jesus and others.
7. We find someone to disciple us.
8. We need to search for someone to mentor us.
9. We discover our spiritual gifts.
10. We find a place to serve within our church community.
11. We take our gifts outside the church walls to the streets to bring healing and salvation to others.
12. We seek Father God, to see if we are to pursue full-time ministry or bring Jesus to others in the marketplace.

Before we came to faith, it was as if we were in a womb, or as the stages of a butterfly in a dark cocoon before popping out and becoming a beautiful creature! But notice those stages here for a butterfly.

- The cocoon
- Breaking out of the cocoon
- Opening and spreading its wings for the first time
- Its first flight
- Servanthood as the butterfly pollinates

There are some interesting parallels between butterflies and followers of Christ.

- Butterflies can stay close to home or fly long distances.
- They can cross-pollinate and help in the reproductive stage of many plants and flowers.
- They are attracted to the eyes of many and are beautiful to look at as they fly, soar and serve.
- As they search for food, they land and perch on large flowers collecting pollen on their legs to take to the next flower that doesn't have enough to survive.
- Butterflies pollinate during the day when flowers are wide open and have a better color perception than bees or humans.
- They find their nectar by being able to see ultraviolet light, which makes flower markings distinct to them.

So, as we see here with a butterfly, so it is with followers of Jesus as we take the love of God, the word of God, and our testimony to those close by as well as distant to bring others to Salvation and healing.

As the butterfly soars so beautifully through the air, it takes pollen to various flowers—close and distant—so it is, as we as followers of Jesus take the gospel spreading the "Good News" to each one we meet.

How do we do this?

- We might offer a kind word or smile.
- God may bring to us someone who needs physical healing, which can become an inroad to share the Gospel.
- Someone might ask us about the Bible, our church, or why we became a Christian.

- We might encounter a homeless person who God tells us to offer food.
- We might take a neighbor's garbage can to the curb or mow their lawn as we mow our own.

No matter what the process is, we are to be spreading the "Good News"/the seed of the Gospel and letting God grow it as we keep on spreading His seed daily.

Let's remember that a farmer doesn't plant a seed to stay up 24/7 watching the seed sprout and then continue to grow. The farmer gets a decent night's sleep so that he can tend to his farm the next day.

Let's also Remember,

As Christians and followers of Jesus, we are only responsible for spreading the seed and praying because everything else is up to God!

God will grow the seed and bring it to fruition as other believers might water that seed, but you and I may never see it come to harvest.

Walk and soar in your identity—your sonship or daughtership in Christ Jesus. The one who gave us His authority to:

- Cast out demons,
- Heal the sick
- Spread the *good news* to all that have ears to hear!

Your new friend,

Pastor Mark

Testimonials

Leon Andrews, *a former board member of* Ramona Vineyard Church, *writes:*

"My wife and I recall Pastor Mark Baxter's sermon series What Are Your Blind Spots? I remember how relevant each sermon was every week as my pastor touched on things in my own life that I didn't look at, and I couldn't and didn't see.

Just as my pastor's analogy of a person driving a car and only seeing what's in the mirrors, missing blind spots, so it is in our own lives as we tend to miss the blind spots that are destroying relationships. Even though we have rearview and side-view mirrors in our vehicles, there are still blind spots that we can't see, and that's why collisions do again happen.

In other words, it's those cars that come speeding up or dart in front of us as we are driving, that we don't see in any of our mirrors; just like when we're going through life's journey, and a blind spot comes in at what seems like out of nowhere from some circumstance.

In each of the Sunday sermons, I began to take an inventory and a severe look at my own life so I could become a better man of God!

Throughout the series, my pastor spoke with authority through Scripture as he also shared real-life experiential stories from his own life as well as from others' life stories concerning blind spots.

I realized first and foremost that we have to be honest with ourselves because we will all eventually have blind spots that will affect all our relationships. As I prayed for God to reveal any of my blind spots in my life, He began to show me visually about my blind spots.

I'm thankful that Pastor Mark heard from the Holy Spirit to bring things to the forefront for our congregation, for how it helped me to be a better man of God, and to see the things that you usually wouldn't see on an everyday basis!

I was encouraged to hear that Pastor Mark was writing a book on this series, which would help the body of Christ.

I'm sincerely thankful to you Pastor Mark for your sermon series, but more than that, for our time together ministering the Gospel to the broken, lonely and lost in Ramona, California."

Erin Williams, *the former Worship Leader at* Ramona Vineyard Church, *writes:*

"I had the privilege to hear the entire series What Are Your Blind Spots? This series ended Pastor Mark Baxter's 26-week series Healing is Relational. I'm most grateful for Pastor Mark's teaching series on blind spots. The entire series helped me to realize how much we need to be in community with other believers to help us see where our blind spots may be. Also, it helped me know how to listen to God and receive feedback from Him and others when they notice a blind spot that we don't see in our own life.

We need to go to Jesus to ask Him to help us to grow in those blind spot areas, so we can walk in victory with Him.

Thank you, Pastor Mark Baxter, for teaching us your insight and wisdom about blind spots!"

Jane Jewell, *a former member of* Ramona Vineyard Church, *writes:*

"While attending Ramona Vineyard Church I was diagnosed with breast cancer and after much prayer, thought and counsel, I made one of the hardest decisions a woman sometimes has to make, and that is to have a double mastectomy. It was all during Pastor

Mark's 12-week series What Are Your Blind Spots? From his 26-week series Healing is Relational.

I'm very thankful for all 12 blind spot sermons, but I'm especially grateful for Pastor Mark's sermons on Fear, and Anxiety & Worry.

After I heard my Pastor preach and teach the two sermons mentioned above from his series What Are Your Blind Spots? I began to see and embrace how someone diagnosed with any disease, might let these two blind spots affect the way one thinks, and acts when a doctor delivers the unwanted news.

I remember when I told Pastor Mark about my diagnosis of cancer; he immediately said to me, the cancer is not mine and that it is a foreign substance, and that it was from the pit of hell.

Pastor Mark immediately put me on a prayer chain. He and a group anointed me with oil, laid hands and prayed over me numerous times throughout my diagnosis, and all the way through surgery too. I remember waking up from surgery seeing my daughter along with Pastor Mark in my recovery room.

Due to Pastor Mark's compassion, words of wisdom, and encouragement, I have shared the same insight with friends that have been diagnosed with diseases to help them find healing and restoration through Jesus.

I'm so thankful that I was able to attend his blind spot series and turn my fear, anxiety and worry over to God, so they didn't turn into blind spots.

Thank you, Pastor Mark Baxter, for your sermon series and especially for always being there through the storms in my life!"

Linda, *a former member of* Ramona Vineyard Church, *from 2012 to 2016, writes.*

"I always enjoyed Pastor Mark Baxter's sermons because they were biblical and spoke to me on a regular basis.

When Pastor Mark began his 26-week series, Healing is Relational; I was excited for each Sunday sermon that continued the series. In the last 12 sermon's What Are Your Blind Spots? I began to see where I had some emotional things going on that the sermon series spoke to that were spot-on in my life.

As he taught about blind spots on Fear, Anxiety & Worry, I began to learn and embrace through the Holy Spirit that I didn't fully trust the Lord in my life.

The Holy Spirit also revealed a blind spot of Anger & Control as I began to see how my joy and peace kept leaving me.

I received prayer up front at the end of each Sunday service that Pastor Mark taught on the blind spots that had taken control of my life.

God continued to reveal why my emotions and actions had gotten somewhat out of control. I read and meditated on the passages of Scripture from the sermons. I kept receiving prayer from ladies on the church prayer team, as-well-as Pastor Mark along with his counsel.

Through spending time with Jesus and His words in Scripture uncovering the lies of Satan, I received the emotional healing I needed. I now trust God with everything in my life, including my entire family.

I also discovered the key to keep my peace and joy, which I truly cherish. Jesus is peace and joy in the fruit of the Spirit in Galatians 5:22-23.

I'm so thankful for the sermon series What Are Your Blind Spots? It helped me to draw closer to Jesus through the work of the Holy Spirit and what Scripture says I am.

I'm so very thankful for your Mark's pastoral care through all the years."

Robert Gonzales, *a former board member of* Ramona Vineyard Church, *writes:*

"I was not just a member of Ramona Vineyard Church in Ramona California, I knew Pastor Mark for many years, heard a plethora of his sermons through *In His Steps Men's and Women's Recovery Homes*, where he taught while I was a resident.

However, none hit home like his 26-week series titled Healing is Relational he taught at our church. When we seem to think we have things under control, suddenly, something comes along that makes us question our walk with Jesus. Well, for me, it was the last 12 sermons from his Healing is Relational series titled What Are Your Blind Spots? These 12 sermons can help us all to deal with multiple issues in everyday life. That is if we humble ourselves to receive it.

My issues started with Fear and Anxiety & Worry and moved on to Anger & Control. At that time in my life, my grandson Jacob was going through some tough times. Jacob was only five going on six years old as he had a ball growing on the bottom of his head inside his skull, which put pressure on his brain. In turn, the force threw off his balance. Anyway, upon receiving this devastating news about Jacob, I immediately confided in Pastor Mark. Afterward, we started praying for him from a distance, and we were even privileged enough to anoint him with oil and lay hands on him several times as Jacob, and his mom visited us at Ramona Vineyard Church in California.

To keep a long story short, I'm praising God for the healing Jacob, as he is doing so much better. Every day the lesion ball shrinks at a slow rate, and nothing tries to attach itself to it.

Pastor Mark's 12-sermon series What Are Your Blind Spots? Helps highlight our blind spots, along with each sermon showing teaching points to help us deal with those revealed blind spots.

Once the Holy Spirit revealed my blind spots, it took trust and faith along with a lot of prayers to get me back on track that put me on the road to freedom in Christ Jesus.

So, for those of you who have chosen to read this book by Pastor Mark, I pray you to get as much out of it as the Lord grants. May each one of you who read with this book be blessed!

I can honestly say that through Pastor Mark, the Lord has blessed me with his knowledge and insight into blind spots that control our lives. Thank you, my friend, my brother in Christ, but mostly my pastor."

Katrina Myhre, *former member of* Ramona Vineyard Church, *writes*:

"My husband and I were blessed to be able to hear the 12 sermons titled What Are Your Blind Spots? That ended Pastor Mark Baxter's 26-week series entitled Healing is Relational. I'm grateful that I listened to the Lord speak to me through those 12 sermons. The Anger & Control sermon spoke to me the most.

Pastor Mark always uploaded his sermons on Facebook, the church website and had previous messages on CD's available on a table everyone saw as they entered the church. I listened to the Anger & Control Blind Spot CD repeatedly!

During the sermon series, I was struggling with an alcoholic husband. Due to the way my spouse treated me, I started carrying quite a bit of anger. I also tried to control the problem myself by forcing my husband to get help for his destructive drinking problem.

The Sunday morning that I heard Pastor Mark's sermon on Anger & Control, I realized that I had allowed a Blind Spot of Anger & Control into my own life. That sermon helped me know that only God can control the situation, and not me. I also realized that it wasn't about my husband, but that it was instead about my relationship with the Lord. Even though I wanted my marriage to work, even worse continued behaviors by my spouse were happening, I ended up having to let him go and divorced him. Thankfully, the Holy Spirit opened the eyes of my heart through the sermons along with Romans 12:1-2, which provided emotional healing for me through that storm of life with my spouse.

A Fear & Anxiety Blind Spot was another one in my life as I got married at 46 years old and now at age 49, I was single and all alone again. The Fear & Anxiety sermon gave me an in-road through life stories that Pastor Mark shared of real experiences him, and others went through in their lives. I realized through the Scripture passages within the sermon that as long as I had my relationship with God, I'm not alone, so there's no reason to live in fear or anxiety anymore.

I'm thankful I was there for all 12 sermons that spoke to me personally. Now that my blind spots got revealed, I was receiving healing as I could soon begin to help my friends, and co-workers with some of their blind spots. Whenever I had the opportunity, I shared my testimony of healing along with offering the blind spot sermon CDs to those that would take time to listen to them.

Thank you, Pastor Mark, for helping me understand my blind spots through the sermons, but more than that, thank you for being available as my pastor to help me walk out the process of healing as well."

Marylin Boecher, *a former member of* Ramona Vineyard Church, *writes:*

"Our church was a small community with large hearts having three pillars: God Loves You, God Accepts You, and God Says You Can't Fail.

I was indeed glad to be there for Pastor Mark Baxter's 26-week series Healing is Relational, as he ended that preaching series with a dynamic 12-week sermon series called What Are Your Blind Spots? When I heard the sermon on the Blind Spot of Offense, I was a bit taken back as I realized there are going to be times where everyone will tend to pick up an offense and hold it against the person that caused it. As Pastor Mark taught on this blind spot, he said there are times in life when people will pick up an offense that isn't even theirs.

In this process, in their minds, those people think they are protecting the person that should receive the attack. Instead, it just means two people are now carrying the same offense. There can also be other times where we don't let go of the offense because of something that stems from either childhood hurts (as we put up walls of protection) or being negatively talked to or about from different people throughout life.

All of Pastor Mark's sermons were recorded, and his blind spot of offense is a listen to for all, so we don't fall into a snare Satan has set. As I listened to my Pastor teach on the blind spot of offense and I allowed the Holy Spirit to take hold of my mind, and my heart, I right then realized this is a blind spot I don't ever want in my life. I most certainly don't ever want to take up an offense that is not mine in the first place.

We all need to allow God to look inside us to help us examine where we are in life with Him. Jesus can massage our hearts, and the Holy Spirit can go to work in us, revealing any, and all blind spots we might have, gently walking us through the restoration process of the relational damage that we caused in our hearts as well as the emotional hurt of others. Through this process, we draw closer to Him as he helps us mend broken relationships in our lives along with Jesus, through the power of the Holy Spirit, bringing healing and revelation of warning in the future for any of these blind spots to arise in our lives. It is all part of the sanctification process that leads us to freedom and produces the fruit to bring us into the character of Christ! *It is for freedom that Christ has set us free. Stand firm, then, and do not let yourselves be burdened again by a yoke of slavery* (Galatians 5:1).

Last, but not least, an excellent thanks to you for always dropping off a CD of the morning sermon when I was under the weather."

Cindy Hasz, LVN, CMC, President/CEO, *Grace Care Management,* writes:

"I was privileged to hear Pastor Mark Baxter's sermon series, What Are Your Blind Spots? It is both compelling, and unique. His sermon series extended over several months when he was my pastor at Ramona Vineyard Church. I was excited when I heard Mark was writing a book that would incorporate the entire 12-week sermon series, and I couldn't wait to read it.

Pastor Mark has a gift of articulating things that other people may avoid but that are important to bring to light. His approach is clear, concise, and easy to apply. In addition to being a good teacher and pastor, he has a gift to bring freedom to the body of Christ by addressing areas that we often don't see and don't know how to deal with.

His teaching and practical steps towards deliverance and healing through the power of the Holy Spirit will bring new life to all those that avail themselves to his wisdom.

Thank you, Pastor Mark, for being led by the Holy Spirit to know what God intended for Ramona Vineyard Church congregation then and for people to read now in your book."

Raymond Twigg, a *former member of* Ramona Vineyard Church *writes:*

"To all who read this book, which I consider a most precious gem in the teachings of God and our Lord Jesus Christ...

I am a Christian, a child of God, lover of Jesus, and His humble follower. I have been walking with and following Him for about three years now. Shortly after giving the steering wheel of my life to Jesus, the Lord opened the door to my wife and me at Ramona Vineyard Church in Ramona, California where our home was. My wife and I attended there for a season.

Pastor Mark Baxter and the Ramona Vineyard Church played a huge part during my Christian infancy as I always-found Pastor Mark's sermons and teachings to be very profound. As I grew to understand the Bible more, I saw how they lined up with the original context in the Bible. I remember how Pastor Mark often quoted one of his professors: All Meaning Is Context Dependent. In other words, I began learning how to exegete (Greek for "take from") a scripture passage rather than eisegesis, which means to read into the Scripture passage what we want it to say.

I also found Pastor Mark's words to be the truth, and the delivery of them hit home with me in an exceptional way. The Holy Spirit moved powerfully at Ramona Vineyard Church every Sunday—from song worship to the sermon, through the altar calls for salvation and prayer for all who needed it. His sermons were inspirational and supported with Scripture. They applied to our walk with Jesus. It quickly became apparent to me that God truly was using this man to further his kingdom and His truth.

My wife and I weren't attending Ramona Vineyard Church for the entire 26-week series; Healing is Relational, by Pastor Mark in 2015. However, we were there for the last 12 sermons of that series, which was called What Are Your Blind Spots? This sermon series spoke volumes to my heart. It proved to be an integral part in understanding the dis-ease I experienced early on, and still do from time to time, being a man of God, walking and living in a fallen world.

Through hearing and applying my pastor's messages regarding blind spots in my life, they all left me with one profound and inspiring reality. I am not perfect.

I soon began to recognize, through Pastor Mark's teaching; that it is by any one of many blind spots that tend to distract me and keep me from God's will for my life.

Not only was I present for Pastor Mark's series on blind spots, but I also made sure I had CD copies of every one of them. I've listened to them repeatedly and still do to this day as I shared them with friends that weren't there to hear the sermons in person. So now, whenever I go through a frustrating time or even doubt, I recognize those moments of apparent separation from God that are of my own making due to a blind spot I did not see coming. I also embrace His grace when it happens.

Pastor Mark, thank you from the bottom of my heart, but more importantly, I thank God that you were a part of my life early on in my walk with Jesus, as a new man of God! And even though I live in California and you now live in Texas, thank you for staying in touch on a regular basis."

About the Author

It was an ordinary day in late June 2016 at 10:00 AM. I was headed home from Starbucks, prepping for Sunday's sermon for my series, "Acronymic Summer." As I drove down Main Street in Ramona all by myself, just chilling and listening to a CD from my previous sermon from Sunday, suddenly, I heard from the Lord as he said this to me: "You are done here in Ramona!" My immediate response was to turn off the CD, and as I did, I felt the Lord say this: "Shut down Ramona Vineyard Church—I'm taking you to Texas."

I immediately began to question God, saying, "Lord, this can't be you! I can't be done here in Ramona because it was you who brought me back to Ramona to plant this church. Besides that, Lord, you know I said I would never move to Texas, so that definitely can't be you speaking to me!" The conversation ended and the voice I heard suddenly went silent.

If you want God to laugh, tell him your plans!

I had to be sure that it was God speaking to me when I began to pray and say, "God, is this is you? Show me!" I continued the drive home very perplexed. I didn't share it with my wife, my church board or anyone in my congregation. For the next three and a half months, I kept what I thought I heard to myself. I began seeking the face of God on this matter and also spent time arguing with Him as I continued to keep what appeared to be a new direction from the Lord close to my heart. As certain events began to unfold, God's words to me in late June had become a reality and were starting to come to fruition.

The first thing that unfolded immediately followed a pastors/leadership conference at Vineyard Anaheim in Anaheim,

California. My worship leader at the time, Hannah Fuentes, got a prophetic word at the meeting. She felt the Lord told her to take a sabbatical from leading worship and to spend more time focusing on just going to church, fellowshipping, and finding out what her new season would become.

Hannah texted me the very next morning and said she wanted a face-to-face with me as she had something important to share with me before the following Sunday. I immediately texted Hannah and asked her to call me on iPhone Face-Time. Right before I answered the Face-Time call, the Holy Spirit told me what Hannah wanted to share. When we connected on Face-Time, I said, "Let me ease your mind and heart, as I know why you needed to talk to me." Hannah was so relieved as she thought that I would see it as her letting me down, but I immediately reassured her. I then told her about God's words to me earlier in late June and that it was just part of His plan for Karen and me to move on, too.

The second event was when one of my board members and his wife, who lived almost an hour away from the church, had been praying and said it was time for them to attend a church closer to home.

The third event that unfolded was when the landlords of our church building emailed me that they were raising our monthly lease significantly. It was more confirmation that God's word in June was now coming to fruition. I went off by myself and spent some time with Abba to get clarification on my next step. In my quiet time, God began laying out his plan for the new season in my wife's and my life. God gave me marching orders with no assignment.

In late June, he had already spoken to me about shutting down the church, and now He was letting me know not to hand the baton to anyone. We were to sell our home and move to Texas. I knew God was laying it all out when the landlord released *Ramona Vineyard Church* from the lease without any financial penalty.

As I began to pray about what to preach for my last sermon, the Lord reminded me of the first sermon I preached when I planted the church. As I prepared the sermon, God began to speak specifics to me. The most important one was that He couldn't do what he wanted to do in each person at *Ramona Vineyard Church,* if Karen and I remained in Ramona.

I preached and shared from my heart on Abram in Genesis 12. God called Abram to leave his home and go to an unknown land. Now, Karen and I were moving to Texas, which was an unknown land to us.

Your new friend,

Pastor Mark

www.ingramcontent.com/pod-product-compliance
Lightning Source LLC
Chambersburg PA
CBHW070550010526
44118CB00012B/1278